THE RAPTURE:

A LOVE STORY

Chuck Mummert

outskirtspress

DENVER, COLORADO

The opinions expressed in this manuscript are solely the opinions of the author and do not represent the opinions or thoughts of the publisher. The author has represented and warranted full ownership and/or legal right to publish all the materials in this book.

BIBLE

Basic **I**nstructions **B**efore **L**eaving **E**arth

We tend to overlook a certain sorrowful moment which occurred within one of the most joyous events in Jesus' ministry. On the very hour of Christ's triumphal Palm Sunday entrance into Jerusalem, when He was being hailed and worshipped as the Messiah by a throng of jubilant believers, ... *when he was come near, he beheld the city and wept over it ... He* [Jesus] *wept because they knew not the time of thy* [His] *visitation,* the time of Messiah's first coming. Even though the Jewish people looked forward to their Messiah's coming, and they had read dozens of prophetic verses concerning this crucial prophetic event, many missed it when it happened. Jesus then predicted horrible judgment and destruction over His beloved Jerusalem because of the spiritual blindness of the majority of His people. (Luke 19:28-44)

Many Christians say they believe in and hope for a Rapture. I have become aware that most really know little about it. The passage above shows that God holds His people responsible for knowing prophetic Scripture and for knowing the time of His visitations. Could history repeat itself? Could He be agonizing over His people today for not being prepared and anxiously anticipating His imminent prophetic visitation—the Rapture?

Preface

The Rapture is an imminent event on God's prophetic calendar. Prophetic scholars point out many end time texts which contain truths relevant to both the Rapture and the Second Coming of Christ. This book primarily focuses upon the Rapture of the Church. Do not confuse the two. At the Rapture, Christ comes as a thief in the night **for** His Church and at the Second Coming, He comes back **with** His Church to earth to reign as the King of Kings over the whole earth for a millennium.

I have been enthralled by this coming event since 1973, when I found myself teaching a prophecy class which was in high demand in a private Christian high school in Denver, Colorado. The staff felt that I was the most qualified to teach prophecy since I had been blessed to sit under Pastor Bob Hooley's ministry for years, and I had graduated from and later taught in a local layman's Bible College. Pastor Hooley truly is one of the most knowledgeable people in the area of prophecy, and has written over a dozen books, booklets, and pamphlets on the subject. [These are available at www.bethelbiblical.org.] Without his depth and spiritual founding, and my wife Norma's dedicated help, I doubt that this book would have ever been written.

This book has a unique organizational approach, which makes it easily understood, while at the same time being very comprehensive in nature. It was created this way because students at the high school were from many different churches and many theological backgrounds; in most cases, however, they had a lack of Biblical teaching altogether. I decided that the best way to approach the topic of the Rapture was to have myself and the students gather all the relevant verses and concepts that they already knew and then organize these into the categories of: *What? How? Where? Why? When?* and *Who?* These are the six questions that every journalist or reporter must answer in order to tell any story or event correctly and completely. In this situation, however, we are discussing a future event of extraordinary importance to believers and nonbelievers alike. Everyone will be greatly affected by it whether they believe in it or not.

The Scriptures related to the **"What," "How,"** and **"Where"** concepts of the Rapture require less analysis and description, so they will be presented first.

Originally, most of the students thought that the **"When"** or the timing (pre-, mid-, post-tribulation) of the Rapture was going to be the most important or the most controversial question; therefore, we will spend significant time on many subtopics of this question. However, as we went through the organizing process, we found that, while extensive, it wasn't the **"When"** Scriptures that were the most important concepts for us to focus on. It was the **"Why"** and the related

"Who" is to be raptured verses and concepts that became the most important and, for some, even more controversial. If that is where Jesus focused most of His Words and parables, it is where we should focus our main attention. The predominant part of the Scriptures and parables given to us on the Rapture focus on the **"Who"** theme. God wants us to focus on the characteristics or heart motivations that are strongly coupled with or wedded to this impending event. These concepts are seldom discussed or emphasized by seasoned Christian believers.

Every Scripture pertinent to this topic of the Rapture that I know of is quoted in this work; well over one-third of this book is pure Scripture (from the King James Version unless otherwise noted). All bolding and underlining within Scriptures are the author's emphasis. The underlined words indicate the characteristics, qualities, or fruits of those who God raptures. A list of all Scriptures used is at the end of the book in the Appendix. If you peruse it at this time, you will see that it is surprisingly extensive. This tells us how important an event the Rapture is in the eyes of God. He must want us to be ready for it!

This book will be quite an eye-opener for all who call themselves Christian, and for those who are simply interested in learning more about such a recognizable but little understood topic as the Rapture. I believe that you, like my classes of students, will experience the life-changing power of the Word of God. It will cause us to make serious attitude and lifestyle changes once we study these Scriptures and truly allow them to penetrate and be infused into our lives.

I've included discussion questions at the back of the book that study groups, Sunday School classes, or thoughtful individuals can use for review and further discussion, as well as reflection and contemplation.

Your Loving Servant,

Chuck Mummert

A person can take a magnifying glass, the strong sun (Son), and focus it just the right distance from an object to start a fire. Your finger can feel the heat in seconds. I found, however, that the right tinder (fuel) is needed. Tissues don't work. Dry paper and wood respond fairly quickly.

If we focus the Son—the Word—correctly, on just the right tinder (a tender heart), a fire can be created in the depth of our souls for our preservation.

Let's Pray Together: God, focus these Scriptures and inspired words into our lives. **Amen.**

Table of Contents

I. WHAT — What is the Rapture?

1 Thessalonians 4:16-18: *[16] For the Lord himself shall descend from heaven with a shout, with the voice of the archangel, and with the trump[et] of God: and the dead in Christ shall rise first: [17] Then we which are alive and remain shall be **caught up** together with them in the clouds, to **meet the Lord** in the air: and so shall we ever be with the Lord. [18] Wherefore comfort one another with these words.* [Note: Bolding and underlining is the author's emphasis.]

This passage speaks of two distinct groups of faithful believers—those who have already died and those who are still alive. For many (the dead in Christ), the Rapture is a resurrection to receive their glorified bodies. For living saints, it is a live removal from this earth up into heaven. The actual word **Rapture** in English is not found in the Bible; it comes from the English translation of the Latin word meaning "caught up," and has become the traditional or historical word used for this imminent event. The word "trinity" is not found either, but the doctrinal importance of both of these truths cannot be denied, especially when one sees how many Scriptures there are on these subjects [see the Appendix for a list of all of the Scriptures related to the Rapture]. The Greek word for *caught up* is **harpazo** [G726 Strong's Concordance], meaning: caught up from one place to another, plucked up, snatched, seized, or taken by force.

The Old Testament will almost always have examples or foreshadows of what will later occur in the New Testament. The Old Testament characters Enoch and Elijah experienced or foreshadowed this type of Biblical happening. Before the time of Noah and the flood judgment, Genesis 5:24 says: *And Enoch <u>walked with God</u>: and he was not; for God took him.* Hebrews 11:5a (NIV—New International Version) further explains: *By faith Enoch was taken from this life, so that he did not experience death; he could not be found.* The King James Version of Hebrews 11:5 says: <u>*By faith,*</u> *Enoch was **translated** that he should not see death; and was not found because God had **translated** him: for before his **translation** he had this testimony, that <u>he pleased God</u>.*

This is the only time that this word *translated* is used in the New Testament; in Greek the word is **metatithemi** [G3346 Strong's Concordance], meaning: transferal (to heaven), transport, exchange, change sides, carry over, remove. Yes, as Hebrews 11:5 says, <u>faith</u> is not only required to believe that God has the power to translate or Rapture someone, but it is also a characteristic or fruit of a person who is raptured; in Enoch's example, the Bible also states that he <u>walked with God</u> and he <u>pleased God</u>.

Concerning Elijah, 2 Kings 2:11(NIV) reads: *As they* [Elijah and his disciple Elisha] *were walking along and talking together, suddenly a chariot of fire and horses of fire appeared and separated the two of them, and Elijah **went up** to heaven in a whirlwind.* Groups or schools of prophets at the two nearby towns of Bethel and Jericho had prophetically been told by God ahead of time of this impending event and warned Elisha twice that Elijah would be taken in such an unprecedented manner (2 Kings 2:3-7). These men so pleased God with their lives that neither Enoch nor Elijah experienced death, but were carried straight into heaven.

You may ask: "Why were these two men so special or so privileged that they didn't have to face death's door?" "Why weren't other Old Testament believers like Abraham or Moses, etc. also spared death?" Since the time of Adam and Eve, the penalty for sin has been death. A better question to ask at this time is why were Enoch and Elijah translated or raptured since they too were born into a sinful nature? It was to give us an Old Testament example of what God planned to do in the future as 1 Corinthians 10:11 (NKJ—New King James Version) says: *Now all these things happened to them as examples and they were written for our admonition, on whom the ends of the ages have come.* Today, most who study prophecy understand that the Church will experience such a snatching away in the near future just as Enoch and Elijah experienced.

The Rapture, the coming of Jesus **for** His saints, should not be confused with His Second Coming **with** His saints at the end of the Great Tribulation; these are different events with different purposes. In the Rapture, Jesus pulls His Church out of this world just before He judges it; at His Second Coming, Jesus returns with His Church after judging this world in order to rule over it during the millennial (1,000 year) reign of Christ on earth. We will rule with Him as "kings and priests" on this earth. Note that in our first Scriptural reference (1 Thessalonians 4:16-18), we meet Christ in the air. He does not come down to the earth and split the Mount of Olives at this time; this occurs at the end of the tribulation at Christ's Second Coming.

The Rapture should not be considered a scary event, but a joyful, blessed, and much anticipated event. Notice that God tells us in 1 Thessalonians 4:18 to comfort each other with these words; **comfort,** which in the original Greek is parakaleo [G3870 Strong's Concordance], is translated to further imply the concept of: to call near, desire, invoke, implore, exhort, beseech, entreat, invite. These are powerful action verbs imploring us to tell others of this coming event. I personally like the translated word "invite" or the idea of an **invitation**—a formal invitation from God to join Him and stay in His home in heaven. He implores us, His Church, to be ready. He yearns for us to come and join Him just like Enoch and Elijah.

Hebrews 10:23-25 says: *²³ Let us hold fast the profession of our faith without wavering; (for he is faithful that promised;) ²⁴ And let us consider one another to provoke [spur (NIV), stir up (RSV—Revised Standard Version)] unto love and to good works: ²⁵ Not forsaking the assembling of ourselves together, as the manner of some is; but exhorting one another: and so much the more, as ye see the day approaching [Day of his coming back again* (Living Bible)].

In contemplating the **"What"** of the Rapture, a person is immediately drawn into thinking about what will immediately happen upon this earth in the seconds and minutes after millions of dedicated Christians are removed in an instant. There will be immediate pandemonium brought to this earth when many pilotless planes and driverless cars and trains and buses crash. Every occupation that a raptured Christian is involved in will suddenly cease, bringing instant tribulation to this world of ours when the Rapture occurs. An instantaneous worldwide tsunami of anarchy and looting of tens of millions of "disappeared" ones' and "left behind" ones' homes and property will ensnare an unwary world. Inspired and encouraged by the lawless spirit of the Lawless One—the Antichrist, worldwide chaos will soon instigate demands for worldwide martial law and a further slide into a one-world government led by the powerful Antichrist who has been waiting to introduce himself to the world. These momentous consequences are what movies could, and have been made about.

II. HOW — How Will the Rapture Be Accomplished?

1 Thessalonians 4:16-17 also explains how this event will occur: *16 For the Lord himself shall descend from heaven with a **shout**, with the voice of the archangel, and with the trump[et] of God: and the dead <u>in Christ</u> shall rise first: 17 Then we which are alive and remain shall be **caught up** together with them in the clouds, to **meet the Lord** in the air: and so shall we ever be with the Lord.* With all of the omnipotent power that God has, when He speaks or shouts, worlds are created and anything can happen.

1 Corinthians 15:35-44 (NIV): *35 But someone will ask, "**How are the dead raised? With what kind of body will they come?**" 36 How foolish! What you sow does not come to life unless it dies. 37 When you sow, you do not plant the body that will be, but just a seed, perhaps of wheat or of something else. 38 But God gives it a body as he has determined, and to each kind of seed he gives its own body. 39 Not all flesh is the same: People have one kind of flesh, animals have another, birds another, and fish another. 40 There are also heavenly bodies and there are earthly bodies; but the splendor of the heavenly bodies is one kind, and the splendor of the earthly bodies is another. 41 The sun has one kind of*

splendor, the moon another, and the stars another; and star differs from star in splendor. [42] *So will it be with the resurrection of the dead. The body that is sown is perishable, it is raised* **imperishable;** [43] *It is sown in dishonor, it is raised in* **glory;** *it is sown in weakness, it is raised in* **power;** [44] *it is sown a natural body, it is raised a* **spiritual body.** *If there is a natural body, there is also a spiritual body.*

Verse 41 states: [one] *star differs from* [another] *star in splendor.* One of the largest stars astronomers have discovered as of the writing of this book is UY Scuti, which is estimated to be 1,700 times bigger than our sun. How could Paul, living in the first century, have known about these differences in size and splendor of the stars without the inspiration of the Holy Spirit in his writing of Scripture. We are just beginning to understand more about this today only because of recent breakthroughs in astronomical technology like the Hubble telescope?

Our old body will be changed! Hallelujah! No more corruption or weakness. Old-timers can really rejoice in this hope and truth! Those with birth defects or lifelong illnesses or bodily weaknesses can rejoice! We will instantly be refashioned with a spiritual body of glory, power, and splendor as God sees fit to reward us.

1 Corinthians 15: 52-58: [52] *In a moment, in the twinkling of an eye, at the last trump: for the trumpet shall sound, and the dead shall be raised incorruptible, and we*

shall be changed. *[53] For this corruptible must put on incorruption, and this mortal must put on immortality. [54] So when this corruptible shall have put on* **incorruption,** *and this mortal shall have put on* **immortality,** *then shall be brought to pass the saying that is written, Death is swallowed up in victory. [55] O death, where is thy sting? O grave, where is thy victory? [56] The sting of death is sin; and the strength of sin is the law. [57] But thanks be to God, which giveth us the victory through our Lord Jesus Christ. [58] Therefore, my beloved brethren, be ye* <u>stedfast, unmoveable, always abounding in the work of the Lord,</u> *forasmuch as ye know that your labour is not in vain in the Lord.*

How can this happen? It will happen in the twinkling of an eye, in a moment, in a flash (NIV) after a shout from our Lord Jesus Christ. He created the whole world by His Word or the authoritative command of His mouth; can He not surely recreate us and our glorious, incorruptible, spiritual body by His shout? Yes, but it takes faith on our part to believe in a resurrection and a Rapture. Don't be like Thomas and doubt, as he doubted Jesus' resurrection body. Only those with a God-given faith will pick up their cross daily and make themselves pure and ready for this special event.

Read the Scriptures concerning Jesus' own resurrection body in Luke 24 and John 20 and 21. At certain times people didn't recognize Him—like the two disciples on the road to Emmaus and, at first, Mary in the garden. However, in most cases His resurrection body was recognizable. Yet he could vanish and appear as he wished. People could touch Him and see the holes in His hands and feet. He could eat, but He probably didn't need to. He fellowshipped with His disciples then, and He so desires to fellowship with all of mankind now.

1 John 3:1-3 (NKJ): *¹ Behold what manner of love the Father has bestowed on us, that we should be called children of God! Therefore the world does not know us, because it did not know him. ² Beloved, now we are children of God; and it has not yet been revealed what we shall be, but we know that when He is revealed, **we shall be like Him,** for we shall see Him as He is. ³ And everyone who has this hope in Him purifies himself, just as He is pure.*

Now arises the million—no, the billion dollar question: What would you give for such a glorious resurrection body that can't become weak, sick, or corrupted by old age? Most of us who have experienced bodily feebleness, infirmity, frailty, and unsightliness would give a lot—no, give every-thing, for a resurrection body. I know that as I age, my desire for a resurrection body grows daily. Ancient explorers like Ponce de León searched their whole life for the Fountain of Youth. Look how much people pay today for plastic surgery or how much time, energy and money people spend trying to improve their looks or their bodies.

What is the spiritual price of such a resurrection body? The answer has already been given in the previous Scriptures;

because of the Father's love, all who are **in Christ** will be given such a body. We can't buy it, earn it, or develop it. **By faith,** Christ will give us this body if we are **in Him.** Salvation is free—it has been paid for in full by Christ's sacrifice on the cross; but it may cost us a lot to follow the Lord. He said that we also would have to pick up our crosses daily as we follow Him.

Hebrews Chapter 11 has been called by many the "faith chapter." It gives a list of many heroes of the faith and all of the challenges they suffered and overcame in order to please and follow God. Verse 35 of that chapter ends with the following statement about why they suffered so faithfully—*that they might* ***obtain a better resurrection.*** These Old Testament saints believed in different levels of resurrection glory or rewards based on our walk down here in this very short life on earth; we will study more about this later.

III. WHERE — Where Will the Rapture Occur?

Is this a silly question or what? Does this aspect of our Rapture topic even need scrutiny? Not so fast. Let's explore this aspect historically.

Originally the Judeo-Christian world, with its Scriptural beliefs, only existed in the tiny land of Israel [roughly one-tenth the size of my state of Colorado or about the size of New Jersey]. If the Rapture had occurred before 35 A.D., it would have happened solely in or very near to Israel.

All early believers were Jews! For a few readers, this may be a surprising statement. Jesus and the early disciples were all Jews. Matthew Chapter 1 gives the Jewish lineage of Jesus back to David and even further back to Abraham to prove his qualifications to be the Jewish Messiah. Jesus was dedicated and circumcised as all Jewish males were on the eighth day (Luke 2:21). He had his bar mitzvah or his spiritual manhood rites in his twelfth year (Luke 2:42) in Jerusalem where He confounded, amazed, and astonished the spiritual leaders of Israel. He attended synagogue regularly (Luke 4:16) and came to the temple in Jerusalem three times a year to celebrate the key Jewish festivals. Jesus ministered almost exclusively to Jews throughout his three years of ministry;

that's why his interactions with the Samaritan and Canaanite women were so unusual (John 4:3-43, Matthew 15:21-28). Jewish culture and law taught them to have nothing to do with Gentiles (non-Jews).

Only after His resurrection did Jesus tell His disciples to go beyond Israel to **all nations** (Matthew 28:19, Mark 16:15). Christ's very last words on earth after His resurrection and before His ascension into heaven were Acts 1:8b: *... and ye shall be witnesses unto me both in Jerusalem, and in all Judaea* (Jewish Israel), *and in Samaria, and unto the* **uttermost part of the earth.** Acts 2:21b: *...whosoever shall call on the name of the Lord shall be saved.*

Because of the Jewish cultural tradition of isolation from the rest of the Gentile world, Peter was given a special vision that had to be repeated three times before it compelled him to reach out to the Gentiles. Acts 10:28b: *...God hath shown me that I should* **not call any man common or unclean.** Acts 10:34-35: *[34] Then Peter opened his mouth, and said, Of a truth I perceive that* **God is no respecter of persons** *[does not show favoritism* (NIV), *shows not partiality* (RSV)]: *[35] But* **in every nation** *he that <u>feareth him</u>, and <u>worketh righteousness</u>, is accepted with him.*

*NOTICE the underlined **"Who"** characteristics or qualifications in this verse: those who fear Him, work righteousness (do what is right—NIV, RSV). Here and throughout the whole book, the underlining is to indicate and emphasize the characteristics of **"Who"** will be raptured. This is an important feature of this book. As you read, focus on these underlined characteristics; they are keys for our culminating and most important topic—the **"Who"**—as well as for our personal lives. [If you scan back over the previous pages, you will find over a dozen underlined characteristics or qualities exhibited by those raptured.]

Later the Holy Spirit was poured out onto these Gentiles (Acts 10:44-47, 11:14-18) as a confirmation of God reaching out to the Gentile world. Paul confirmed this when he said that his ministry was first to the Jews and then to the Gentiles. Within a short time, believers came to be known as "Christians," first in Antioch—300 miles north of Jerusalem on the Syrian-Turkish border. No longer was Christianity just an offshoot of Judaism, but it was becoming a worldwide religion. The Jewish prophet Isaiah was correct when he prophesied several times that the light of the Jewish nation would enlighten the whole Gentile world. Isaiah 49:6b (RSV): *...I will give you as a light to the nations, that my salvation may reach to the end of the earth.* Isaiah 49:22a (RSV): *Thus says the Lord God: "Behold, I will lift up my hand to the nations, and raise my signal to the peoples;"* Other references from Isaiah concerning the Gentiles are found in: Isaiah 11:10, 42:1 and 6, 60:3, 62:2, 66:19, and all of Chapter 56.

Revelation 5:9b: [He has]...*redeemed us to God by thy*

blood out of every kindred [tribe], *and tongue, and people, and nation;*

These verses make it clear that the Rapture is going to oc-cur **everywhere** on earth where there are faithful Christians. No, you do not have to relocate to be part of this key event. The Rapture is not restricted to any tribe, nation, ethnic group, race, denomination, or people on earth. God the Father is searching the byways of this whole globe for a people (Luke 14:21-23). For further Scriptures on this concept, study the following: Luke 3:6, Romans 5:18, 1 Timothy 2:4, Titus 2:11, 2 Peter 3:9.

IV. WHY — Two Reasons Why There Will Be a Rapture

A Love Story of the Bride

Now to explain why the subtitle of this book is *A Love Story* and delve into greater spiritual depth concerning our subject.

What is your relationship with God? How do you perceive Him? Is He just a distant powerful entity that you may occasionally pay homage to in some religious fashion or ceremony? Christianity is not just a religion; Christ wants us to have a close personal fellowship with Him. God wants to take you deeper in His relationship with you. That's why *Jesus said unto him* [us], *Thou shall **love the Lord thy God** **with all thy heart, and with all thy soul, and with all thy mind.** This is the first and great commandment.* (Matthew 22:37-38). He wants to be Lord and King on the throne of your heart and life. He wants to be the **Father** as you crawl up in His lap as the **children** and **heirs** of God (Romans 8:15-17). God wants not only to be your Father, but your **friend** as you grow in Him (John 15:14-15). Then He wants you to realize and take a step ever closer—even more intimate in Him. In many places, Scripture calls the true Church the **Bride of Christ**. One reason for the Rapture is that Christ will gather

His beloved **Bride** into heaven for the Marriage Supper of the Lamb. I believe that for many—maybe most people, this might be a new revelation or understanding of this event. Christ's love and desire is for His Bride—the Church, and He desires for us to have that type of love relationship with Him.

This is the same type of relationship that God wanted to have with His Jewish people, and in the end He will have it with them. The Almighty God also said of the Jewish faithful that He is *married unto you* (Jeremiah 3:14), that He is *thine husband* (Isaiah 54:5), and that *I will betroth you to Me forever; Yes, I will betroth you to Me In righteousness and justice, in loving-kindness and mercy; I will betroth you to Me in faithfulness, and you shall <u>know the Lord</u>* (Hosea 2:19-20 NKJ). As He loves the Church, so too He has a special love for the Jewish people. He has always desired a personal love relationship with His people here on earth and throughout all of eternity.

The above concept of God's love for the Jewish people may be new to some, as is the following which is vital in fully comprehending the Rapture. Notice how **Christ** is spoken of as being **the Bridegroom** by John the Baptist, by Jesus himself, and by Christ's disciples and followers. In John 3:28b-30 (NIV), John the Baptist said: [28b] ..."*I am not the Messiah but I am sent ahead of him.*" [29] *The bride belongs to the **bridegroom**. The friend who attends the bridegroom <u>waits and listens for him</u>, and is full of joy when he hears the bridegroom's voice. That joy is mine, and it is now complete.*

[30] *He must become greater; I must become less.*

Jesus says that He's the **Bridegroom** in Matthew 9:14-15 (NIV) [also Mark 2:18-20 and Luke 5:33-35]: *[14] Then John's [the Baptist's] disciples came and asked him [Jesus], "how is it that we and the Pharisees fast often, but your disciples do not fast?" [15] **Jesus** answered, "How can the guests of **the bridegroom** mourn while he is with them? The time will come when the **bridegroom** will be taken from them; then they will fast."*

Furthermore, Paul identifies Christ as **the Bridegroom** when speaking to the early Church in Romans 7:4 (Living): *Your "husband," your master, used to be the Jewish law; but you "died" as it were, with Christ on the cross; and since you are" dead," you are no longer "married to the law," and it has no more control over you. Then you came back to life again when Christ did, and are a <u>new person</u>. And now you are "**married**" so to speak, to [Christ] the one who rose from the dead, so that you can <u>produce good fruit</u>, that is, <u>good deeds</u> for God.*

This Bride concept isn't meant to be sexual in nature; it represents becoming one with and having the strongest and closest love relationship possible. The Jewish religious sect called the Sadducees, who didn't believe in resurrection, was also wrong in their earthly thinking about heavenly marriage. When they tried to trick Jesus with a question about who would be married to whom in heaven, *Jesus answered and said unto them* in Matthew 22:29: *Ye do err, not knowing the scriptures, nor the power of God.*

Galatians 3:26, 28-29 (NKJ): [26] *For you are all sons of God through faith in Christ Jesus...* [28] *There is neither Jew nor Greek, there is neither slave nor free, there is neither male nor female; for you are all one in Christ Jesus.* [29] *And if you are Christ's, then you are Abraham's seed, and heirs according to the promise.* For many men, the concept of us being the Bride of Christ is hard to comprehend; we have to understand that in heaven there will be no sexual difference between men and women. Even though we may dearly love our mates here on earth, our marriage is not to other people in heaven, but unto Christ.

2 Corinthians 11:2 (NIV): *I am jealous for you with a godly jealousy. I promised you to one **husband, to Christ,** so that I might present you as a pure virgin to him.* This means we must reserve our bodies, souls, minds, and hearts for Christ alone.

Ephesians 5:25-27, 32: [25] *Husbands, love your wives, even as Christ also loved the church, and gave himself for it;* [26] *That he might sanctify and cleanse it with the washing of water by the word,* [27] *That he might present it to himself a glorious church, not having spot, or wrinkle, or any such thing; but that it should be holy and without blemish.* Paul then speaks of Christ—the Bridegroom and His relationship with the Church as a **great mystery.** I love a mystery, don't you? [32] *This is a great mystery: but I speak concerning Christ and the church.* In mysteries, we can't wait to see "who" was involved and to see everything explained, solved, and wrapped up. This book will help.

John 14:1-3: *¹ Let not your heart be troubled: ye believe in God, believe also in me. ² In my Father's house are many mansions* [rooms, abodes, residences]: *if it were not so, I would have told you. I go to prepare a place for you. ³ And if I go and prepare a place for you, I will come again, and receive you unto myself; that where I am, there ye may be also.*

Jesus at this time is preparing mansions (or an abode, rooms) for His Bride, and He longs to return and receive His Bride unto Himself. *Eye hath not seen, nor ear heard, neither have entered into the heart of man, the things which God hath prepared for them that <u>love him</u>* (1 Corinthians 2:9).

Revelation 19:7-9: *⁷ Let us be glad and rejoice, and give honour to him: for the **marriage of the Lamb** [Jesus] is come, and his **wife** [the Church] <u>**hath made herself ready.**</u> ⁸ And to her was granted that she should be arrayed in fine linen, clean and white: for the fine linen is the <u>righteousness</u> of saints. ⁹ And he saith unto me, Write, Blessed are they which are called unto the **marriage supper of the Lamb.** And he saith unto me, These are the true sayings of God.*

Notice in Revelation that even the dress (our righteousness) is granted or given to us—the Bride. We can't make it ourselves, as my wife made her wedding dress, or buy it as many modern brides do. After they sinned, Adam and Eve tried to clothe themselves in their own garments made of fig leaves; but it took a sacrifice provided by God to cover them. For us today, it is God who makes us righteous by the sacrifice of His Son.

He has made it possible for us to be clean, holy, without spot or wrinkle, and without blemish through the sacrifice of His Blood and the washing of His Word. We have to do our part, however. We are to "examine ourselves" daily and especially when we drink of the communion cup (1 Corinthians 11:28). If we see spots of shame on our wedding garments, we must strip ourselves and clean the spots and iron the wrinkles. We are to make ourselves ready, and we are to keep ourselves spotless and prepared.

Our Biblical Roots Concerning Betrothal And Marriage Traditions

To better understand our Bible and the key concept of why there will be a Rapture, it is very illuminating and important that we obtain an understanding of our Jewish roots or the religion, culture, and the traditions that our Old Testament and New Testament were created from. Concerning the concept of the Rapture and the Bride of Christ, it is very helpful to understand Eastern/Middle Eastern or Biblical betrothal or marriage traditions.

I have taught the following concepts in church sermons, specialized classes for a layman's Bible College, and "Our Jewish Roots" seminars. My main 34-year career in public education was teaching world geography and history with some government and economics. The following is a brief scholastic summary of Eastern Hemisphere culture (Africa,

Middle East, Far East), especially focusing on Old Testament Jewish wedding customs. Although these practices differ according to time and place, many of these cultural customs can still be found even today throughout more traditional world cultures.

Family practices in the Eastern hemisphere or more traditional cultures are very different from modern American/ European or "western" cultures. Biblical lifestyle was based on many of these Eastern traditional practices. Below are some basic differences concerning family practices—however, not all of these concepts apply to all cultural areas in the world; for example, modern urban areas, even though in the East, are being greatly affected by more modern or "western" culture and tend to be less traditional.

- They practice an "extended family" system, not a "nuclear family" system; this means that the bride and groom do not set up their own house. The bride goes to live with the groom's large extended family which may include grandparents, parents, uncles, aunts, cousins, etc.

- This is a patriarchal system; the oldest male rules over the family. However, often the oldest female rules over household matters.

- In the Jewish culture, women are respected and highly protected.

- Dating isn't usually allowed and young women are to be discreet and stay in protected family circles.

- Marriages are arranged by the fathers of the bride and groom; however, in the Jewish culture, the bride must also give her consent to the marriage.

- Extensive dowry (money, jewelry, cattle, and/or labor for the bride paid to her father) is still practiced. Study the Old Testament examples of Rebekah (Genesis 24), Rachel (Genesis 29:16-30), and Dinah (Genesis 34:3-12).

- Betrothal, once agreed on by all parties, is considered to be a legally binding marriage contract. However, couples do **not** live together at this point and may not even be allowed to see each other.

Carefully examine the following concepts and see how they are a beautiful example of the Church's marriage to Christ. See how much you can glean from these practices and apply them to your spiritual walk today. To do this, it would be helpful to look up the related New Testament Scriptures. Once familiar with these betrothal and marriage customs, you will also comprehend our later discussion of Christ's parables in a much fuller way. You will also further understand how Jesus sees you as His Bride and He desires, no—requires, a deeper love relationship with you.

Eastern and Jewish Wedding Customs

[For this section alone, italics denotes either Biblical quotes or the correlating concept to the Church]

A. Betrothal Phase

   1. Contract made:

      a. The bridegroom, the fathers and two witnesses meet. *[John 3:16: The Father initiated the sending of His Son.]*

      b. The agreed-on legal document containing the conditions of marriage is signed. *[Hebrews 9: 7, 12, 22: It took Christ's blood sacrifice to redeem us. Matthew 26:28-29: "this is my blood of the new testament...I will not drink...of this... until that day when I drink it new with you in my Father's kingdom."]*

   2. The bride price or dowry is paid by the groom to the bride's father. *[1 Peter 1:18-19 (Living): [18]"God paid a ransom to save you...not mere gold or silver... [19] But he paid for you with the precious life blood of Christ..."]*

   3. A special cup of wine, or the "cup of acceptance," is poured by the bridegroom for the bride.

      a. The bride can accept or reject the betrothal—drink or reject the cup of wine. *[Symbolic of communion—John 1:12, Romans 10:9: we must choose to accept and <u>con-fess our acceptance</u>. Genesis 24:58: Rebekah had to accept Eliezer's proposal with "I will" or "I do." 1 Corinthians 10:16a: "The cup of blessing which we bless, is it not the communion of the blood of Christ?"]*

      b. Gifts are given to the bride. *[Acts 2:38-39, 1 Corinthians 12:1-11: Gifts of the Holy Spirit.]*

      c. While legally married at this point, the couple does not live together for a considerable period of time. *[John 3:28-29, Matthew 9:15: Jesus is called the Bridegroom and the Church is called His <u>Bride</u> even* *though we are not with him. Matthew 1:18-19:* [18] *"... When as his mother Mary was espoused to Joseph, before they came together* (in sexual consummation), *she was found with child of the Holy Ghost.* [19] *Then Joseph, her husband, being a just man, and not willing to make her a public example, was minded to put her away privily"* (divorce).]

4. The groom separates from the bride and prepares the wedding chamber.

   a. This is usually added onto the father's house (extended family) *[John 14:2-3 (NIV):* [2] *"My father's house has many rooms... I am going there to prepare a place for you.* [3] *...I will come back and take you to be with me..."]*

   b. The groom doesn't see the bride during construction. *[2 Corinthians 5:7: "We walk by faith, not by sight" in the blessed hope. 1 Peter 1:8 (Living): "You <u>love him</u> even though you have never seen him; though not seeing him, you <u>trust him</u>; and even now you are happy with the inexpressible joy that comes from heaven itself."]*

   c. The father decides the exact timing of the wedding (the bridegroom and bride don't know it). *[Mark 13:32-37, Matthew 24:36: But of that day and that hour knoweth no man...but the Father only; Matthew 24:44, 25:13.]*

5. While separated, the bride <u>prepares</u> for the groom. *[2 Corinthians 11:2: "...I have espoused* (married) *you... that I may present you as a chaste virgin to Christ."]*

   a. The bride takes a [mikveh], an immersed cleansing bath. *[Water baptism—2 Corinthians 7:1; Romans 6:3-6: We are buried with him by water baptism into death and raised from the dead into life. We are also <u>washed by His Word</u>: John 15:3; Ephesians 5:26.]*

   b. The bride uses the gifts given to her by the groom to prepare herself. *[2 Timothy 1:6; 1 Corinthians 14:1,*

12: Stir up, desire, be zealous for, seek after that ye may excel in spiritual gifts.]

c. The bride prepares her wedding garments and makes herself ready. *[Revelation 16:15 and 19:7-9; Ephesians 5:25-27: be holy, not having spots or wrinkles.]*

d. The bride is to be veiled if in public *[2 Corinthians 6:14-18: Be not yoked together with unbelievers... come out from among them, be ye separate from the world.]*

e. The bride is called by others: "bought with a price," "dedicated to another," "set apart," "consecrated," "drunk the cup," "separate from the world" *[1 Corinthians 6:20, 7:23: "we are bought with a price."]*

f. The bride's focus and future expectation is totally on preparing for life with her future groom; she waits, watches, looks for and anticipates his coming for her. *[Betrothed people dream of, think daily of, write to and want to read love letters from and talk to their beloved future mates; we must guard against losing our first love type of relationship, Revelation 2:4: Read and reread His letters (Bible) and yearn to talk to Him daily (prayer).]*

g. Oil is put into the lamp daily—the lamp is lit and put in the window for all to see as a confirmation of her covenant. *[Lamp put in window to mark her place and faithfulness. Matthew 25:1-13, Matthew 5:14-16: Ye are the light of the world, Proverbs 13:9, Psalms 119:105 (oil is symbolic of the Holy Spirit).]* Note: An example of this small lamp is on the back cover of this book on top of the Bible—our love letters.

B. Wedding and Celebration Phase

1. The groom comes for his bride.

a. Groom and friends come, usually after midnight (dark times), in a noisy procession of candles or lit lamps. *[1 Thessalonians 4:16-18, 5:2: He comes as a "thief in the night" with a shout and the voice of the archangel and the trumpet of God.]*

b. The trumpet [shofar] sounds and the groom shouts.

c. He steals away his bride (as a thief) by candlelight; the bride is said to be "stolen," "caught up," "snatched away." It is my understanding that the bridegroom even has the right to leave behind an unprepared or unfaithful bride. *[1 Thessalonians 5:1-8, Revelation 3:2-3, 10-11. He comes as a thief in the night and we are told to <u>watch</u> and <u>not be asleep</u>, to be <u>sober, persevere, hold fast, having faith and love.</u>]*

2. Consummating the Marriage

   a. There is a long (seven-day) celebration with family and friends—"fulfilling her week."

   b. Sealing the covenant—breaking the hymen. *[We are to be virgins—only have our relationship with Christ, not with this world; Revelation 19:7: "...the marriage of the lamb is come, and his wife hath <u>made herself ready.</u>"]*

   c. The best man waves the sheet as proof of virginity and faithfulness.

   d. The couple takes food together. *[Heavenly communion, Matthew 26:26-29.]*

   e. As loving couples do—they call each other by special loving names. *[Christ will give each member of the Bride a special personal new name, Rev. 2:17 and 3:12.]*

3. Marriage Feast—supper—the bride is accepted into the groom's father's family. *[Ephesians 2:11-22 and 3:1-9: There is a uniting of Old and New Testament saints. Ephesians 2:13-19 says: "But now in Christ..." "made both one..." "the twain one..." "reconciles both unto God..." "fellow citizens with the saints, and of the household of God."]*

This study is one reason why I gave this book the title *The Rapture: A Love Story*. Now that you have ventured this far with me, and if you feel that you are desirous of or will be attending Christ's wedding feast, then your *Heavenly Wedding Invitation* can be found on page 28. Remember that 1 Thessalonians 4:18 says to *"comfort one another with these words"*; comfort means to **invite,** invoke, provoke, implore, beseech one another.

If you have never accepted the Father's gift of salvation through His Son's sacrifice for you, then simply pray and ask Jesus to forgive you of your sins and come into your life and help make you into the loving bride as we have outlined above and throughout this book.

Credits for Eastern and Jewish Wedding Customs section:

James M. Freeman, *Manners and Customs of the Bible*, Logos Int'l., 1972, ISBN 0-88270-022-7, pp. 15, 26, 32, 37-38, 60, 282, 376-379.

Abraham Chill, *The Mitzvot,* Keter Publishing House, Jerusalem, Ltd., 1990, ISBN 0-7065-1463-7, pp. 64-66, and 458-460.

Richard Booker, *Here Comes the Bride,* Sounds of the Trumpet, 1995, ISBN 0-9615302-4-3, pp. 1-12, 23-31, and 35-41.

Mark Biltz, *The Feasts of the Lord* (workbook), El Shaddai Ministries, 2008, pp. 27-32.

HEAVENLY WEDDING INVITATION

The Father invites YOU

To the Wedding and Marriage Supper of His Son,
the Lamb, the Loving Messiah, the King of Kings

This marriage is to the lovely and adopted
Bride of Christ
Who is prepared and has made herself ready

Following will be an elaborate and lengthy Wedding Supper
In His prepared place in Heaven

Even though delayed, it will be SOON
Exact time to be determined by the Father
He will pick you up in His ultimate stretch limo (called the fiery chariot),
So you must be ready at all times
It is so worth the wait—WATCH and keep your lamps lit!

Attire: Formal white(s)—clean, without spot or wrinkle

Admission has already been paid for in full by the Son's sacrifice

Presents are not needed since God owns everything
Present only Yourself, with all the love for the Father and His Son

Other guests are welcome.
The Father is so rich and loving that He implores you
to invite all you know to join the other saints
as long as they respect the admission, the dress, and the heart requirements.

What a wedding! What a party! What an eternity! Don't miss it!

"Eye hath not seen, nor ear heard, neither have entered into the heart
of man, the things which God hath prepared for them that love him."
[1 Cor. 2:9]

Separation From the Indignation and Judgment of the Lord

Thus far, we have examined only one reason for the Rapture—the gathering of Christ's beloved Bride into heaven for the Marriage Supper of the Lamb. There is, I believe, a second major reason why God gathers in His people, and it is connected to the timing of the Great Tribulation judgment. It is at this point in the progression and organization of this book, that I can no longer keep two subdivisions separate; the **"Why"** and the **"When"** have to be, at least in part, discussed together. It is also where I must apprise you that I believe the Rapture and the beginning of the Great Tribulation are basically simultaneous. While it is a glorious happening for the Church, it is horrendous for this world for reasons that we have already briefly mentioned. Matthew 24:21: *For then shall be great tribulation, such as was not since the beginning of the world to this time, no, nor ever shall be.* Instant destruction, chaos, and anarchy will break out. As you will see in the **"When"** section, the Anti-Christ will be unleashed on the earth. Christ's beloved and righteous Bride is not to be judged with this world during God's Great Tribulation judgment of this earth.

For now, let's continue in the Old Testament realm of Scriptures and foreshadowing examples. Further New Testament Scriptures, reasoning, and proofs for my and others' pre-tribulation belief will follow toward the end of the **"When"** unit of study. Besides the two Old Testament examples of Enoch and Elijah who were "caught up" to heaven without experiencing death, the Old Testament might be speaking to the question of **why** there will be a special event called the Rapture in Isaiah 26:19-21 which says: *[19] Thy dead men shall live, together with my dead body shall they arise. Awake and sing, ye that dwell in dust: for thy dew is as the dew of herbs, and the earth shall cast out the dead. [20] **Come, my people,** enter thou into thy chambers, and shut thy doors about thee: **hide thyself** as it were for a little moment, until the **indignation be overpast.** [21] For, behold, the LORD cometh out of his place to punish the inhabitants of the earth for their iniquity: the earth also shall disclose her blood, and shall no more cover her slain.*

In verse 19, we see an Old Testament Scripture concerning the resurrection of the dead, and it continues on in verse 20 with a Scripture on God's **indignation** [H2195 Strong's Concordance—God's fury, rage, anger] and the resulting judgment, which I believe is referring to the seven-year period of Great Tribulation. His people are told to come into His prepared chambers and hide until the indignation has passed over. I believe the chambers to be those God is preparing for us in heaven (spoken of earlier in John 14:1-3). The indignation is the seven years of Great Tribulation during which pre-tribulation Christians believe that the Church will be in heaven at the marriage supper with Christ. God won't allow His faithful, beloved Church to be judged with this unrighteous world as God pours out His judgment during the Great Tribulation. However, it is believed by many that during this time, the Church will be judged by Christ for rewards at His [bema] judgment seat; this is a judgment for rewards or commendation, not condemnation. [This is not the Great White Throne Judgment of Revelation 20:11-15 at the end of times for lost souls.] Then He will return at the end of the Great Tribulation at His Second Coming (Revelation 19) **with** the Church to set up His millennial reign or kingdom on earth. Revelation 19:11-14 says that after the marriage of the Lamb, then heaven opens and Jesus returns from heaven riding a white horse **with** His armies of heaven (the Church) also riding white horses and clothed in fine white linen.

To the humble and obedient there is a conditional message given to Zephaniah in Chapter 2 verses 2-3 (Living): [2] *while there still is time—before judgment begins, and your opportunity is blown away like chaff; before the fierce anger of the Lord falls and the terrible day of his wrath begins.* [3] *Beg him to save you, all who are <u>humble</u>—all who have tried to <u>obey</u>. <u>Walk humbly and do what is right</u>; perhaps even yet the Lord will protect you from his wrath in that day of doom.*

The two reasons **why** there will be a Rapture are seen in the very nature of God our Father. His great **love** for us—the faithful Bride for His Son and for the world—must also be balanced with the inevitable need for **justice** on this earth. This need for justice has been building up and getting worse over the decades and centuries; justice will follow during the seven years of Great Tribulation on this earth.

Psalm 89:14 (NIV) says: ***Righteousness and justice are the foundation of your throne; love and faithfulness go before you.***

What examples can you think of in the Old Testament where God directly judged this world (or part of it) for its extraordinary level of depravity and sinfulness? This is done in order to stop the continual process of more and more generations of lost souls being propagated into this world only to be easily overwhelmed by a uniform or homogeneous society subverted by sin, debauchery, and spiritual darkness.

Romans 11:22a (Living): *Notice how God is both kind and severe. He is very hard on those who disobey, but very good to you if you continue to <u>love</u> and <u>trust</u> him...*

It has been said that Old Testament Jews may have overemphasized the concepts of God's justice and judgment, while New Testament Christians have overemphasized the concepts of God's love and mercy. God has a perfect balance of both love and justice. Didn't the Father's righteous justice and love for mankind cause Him to have to send His Son to die and fulfill the needed blood sacrifice required to redeem the human race? Doesn't God want us to walk in a balance of love and righteous fear (or reverence) of Him?

Deuteronomy 10:12-13 (NIV) says: [12] *...what does the Lord your God ask of you but to **fear** the Lord your God, to walk in obedience to him, to **love** him, to <u>serve</u> the Lord your God with all your heart and with all your soul, [13] and to* *observe* the Lord's commands and decrees that I am giving you today for your own good? No matter if you believe in a pre-, mid-, or post-tribulation Rapture, the concept of God's agape love and His righteous judgment of this earth come together in these two concurrent events—the Rapture and the seven years of Great Tribulation.

There is more proof of this concept to be found in Old Testament foreshadowing, or types and shadows, for: *[11] Now all these things happened unto them* [Old Testament saints] *for examples: and they are written for our admonition, upon whom the **ends of the world are come**. [12] Wherefore let him that thinketh he standeth take heed lest he fall* (1 Corinthians 10:11-12).

What does foreshadowing mean? *Webster's Dictionary* defines foreshadowing as: *to show or indicate beforehand; prefigure.* Imagine a person with the sun behind him. In front of him or before him is cast a shadow or an outline of himself, but it is just a dark form or an outline of himself.

Similarly, things that God wrote about in the Old Testament were principles or patterns of something greater to come. For example, Israel's mobile tabernacle and later their exalted temple are things that God gave a lot of instructions, exact patterns, and directions for, yet Scripture says they are still only shadows of greater heavenly truths and things to come.

The Almighty God also gave exact instructions and details concerning the feasts or special high holidays that He wanted His Jewish people to celebrate. The timing of these was exact. Christ has already completely fulfilled all three of the spring feasts in His death, burial, and resurrection at His First Coming. God has also fulfilled the summer feast of Pentecost with the pouring out of the Holy Spirit on the day of Pentecost. Having done this, God will also fulfill all three of the fall feasts in the three future events of the Rapture, the Great Tribulation, and the Second Coming.

Abraham's life story gives us a perfect foreshadowing example of God separating His righteous people out from His judgment. When Abraham learned of the impending judgment of God to come on Sodom and Gomorrah, he interceded with God for his nephew Lot who was in Sodom. Genesis 18:23 and 25 (NKJ) read: ²³ *And Abraham came near and said,* **Would you also destroy the righteous with the wicked?** ²⁵ *Far be it from You to do such a thing as this, to slay the righteous with the wicked, so that the righteous should be as the wicked; Far be it from You!* **Shall not the Judge of all the earth do right?**

Abraham knew his God just as the Psalmist did when he wrote Psalm 97:2b: *...righteousness and judgment are the habitation of his throne.* Psalm 96:10b and 13: ^{10b} *...**he shall judge the people righteously.** ¹³ for he cometh to judge the earth: he shall judge the world with righteousness...*

God, the righteous judge, agreed with Abraham's argument. God agreed that He wouldn't judge Sodom if there were even ten righteous people in the city (Genesis 18:32)—but there weren't ten. Lot hadn't been a faithful or fruitful light to his city. This is a warning to us. Instead, the city's corrupt culture had slowly **vexed** Lot. 2 Peter 2:6-8 says: *⁶ And turning the cities of Sodom and Gomorrha into ashes condemned them with an overthrow, making them an example unto those that after should live ungodly; ⁷ And delivered just Lot, **vexed** with the filthy conversation (lifestyle) of the wicked: ⁸ (For that righteous man dwelling among them, in seeing and hearing, **vexed** his righteous soul from day to day with their unlawful deeds;)*

What a lesson for us today! We need to be careful about what we open our lives to, lest we, like Lot, become **vexed** [H928 & G2669 Strong's Concordance—oppressed, worn down, sink to the bottom, tormented, tortured]. Ezekiel 16:49-50 further explains to us that Sodom's key sins were pride, fullness of bread, idleness, haughtiness and the abominations of sexual perversion. Their sins sound very much like our nation today; we too can become and are becoming vexed and hardened by all we see and hear around us. Spiritual filth and rot bombards us daily without us even trying to search it out.

If you are thinking that this is just an irrelevant Old Testament story, Jesus himself, in Luke 17:32, says that we (the Church) are to learn from and **Remember Lot's**

wife! She was so vexed and desirous of Sodom's lifestyle that she disobeyed God and lovingly looked back one more time at Sodom where her heart was. When God desired deliverance for her, she disobeyed and was destroyed along with Sodom's judgment and destruction. Jesus said in Luke 9:62 that you cannot plow a straight furrow looking back; you must keep your focus on a distant goal ahead to keep on the straight and narrow. Matthew 7:13-14 (NIV): *[13] Enter through the narrow gate. For wide is the gate and broad is the road that leads to destruction, and many enter through it. [14] But small is the gate and narrow the road that leads to life, and only a few find it.* Lot was miraculously plucked safely out of sudden destruction, and yet Lot's disobedient wife, because of a worldly heart, wasn't saved from devastation. Two were called out, but only one was taken. It was God who judged their hearts and actions. He knows our actions as well as the thoughts and intents of our hearts.

Israel's deliverance from Egypt gives us another example of this same truth. In God's eternal plan to remove His people Israel from slavery and destruction in Egypt, He began to bring many judgments or plagues on the Egyptians. We are told six times (Exodus 8:22-23, 9:4-6, 9:26, 10:23, 11:7 and 12:23) that God protected His Jewish people from the plagues which were in their area called Goshen. The last plague or judgment that came upon the Egyptians was the death of the firstborn. God, however, made a way of escape for His obedient and faithful people who followed His directions by sacrificing the Passover lamb and placing its blood over the doorposts of their homes. He then led them out miraculously toward their promised land.

These are foreshadowing examples given to us from God's Old Testament of two men raptured into heaven, and examples of God's faithful people being delivered from God's unprecedented judgments on this wicked world. They are placed in the Bible for our admonition, example, and inspiration. These are character studies that give us lessons about the characteristics of those **"Who"** will be snatched away. I believe that they indicate a pre-tribulation Rapture before the judgment of God on the earth; they also speak to us about the challenges of lifestyle conditions that we face today.

V. WHEN — Truths Concerning the Timing of the Rapture

Jesus is coming soon! What thoughts come into your mind when you read or hear this? Be honest with yourself. If this doesn't cause a bride-like excitement in your heart, then it's time to stir yourself up in the Lord! What if you believed that He is coming in one month from now—or tomorrow? How would you respond? Would the routines and cares of this life matter anymore? How would you change your life? What would you do first? Who would you tell?

Date setting for the Rapture or the Second Coming of Christ as done by various people, especially cult groups, is totally unscriptural and has brought ridicule to the Church by the world. As we approach the soon-coming Rapture, I believe we are being distracted from the more important concept of **who** will be raptured with the less important concept of **when** the Rapture will occur.

Our key chapter concerning issues around the timing or the **"When"** of the Rapture, which we will carefully dissect in the next few sections, is found in **Matthew 24** (and **Mark 13**). There are over half a dozen concepts that we can learn about concerning the timing of the Rapture and we will cover each one of them in the following sections as we study Matthew 24.

No One Knows the Day nor Hour Except the Father

Let's begin with Matthew 24:36 and 42 (NKJ): *[36] But of that day and hour no one knows, no, not even the angels of heaven, but My Father only. [42] <u>Watch</u> therefore, for you do not know what hour your Lord is coming.*

Mark 13:32-37: *[32] But of that day and **that hour knoweth no man**, no, **not the angels** which are in heaven, **neither the Son,** but the Father. [33] <u>Take ye heed,</u> <u>watch</u> and <u>pray:</u> for ye know not when the time is. [34] For the Son of man is as a man taking a far journey, who left his house, and gave authority to his <u>servants,</u> and to every man his <u>work,</u> and commanded the porter to <u>watch.</u> [35] <u>Watch</u> ye therefore: for ye know not when the master of the house cometh, at even, or at midnight, or at the cockcrowing, or in the morning: [36] Lest coming suddenly he find you sleeping. [37] And what I say unto you I say unto all, <u>Watch.</u>*

Matthew 25:13: *<u>Watch</u> therefore, for **ye know neither the day nor the hour** wherein the Son of man cometh.*

Notice that we are given a list of things that God wants His faithful to be doing: we are to <u>take heed,</u> <u>pray,</u> <u>serve,</u> <u>work,</u> and many times we are told to <u>watch;</u> we will explore the watch concept in more detail in the last portion of this book.

The all-important final conclusion that we must absolutely understand concerning **"When"** is: *that day nor hour knoweth no man but the Father.* In the Old Testament Jewish wedding tradition that we just studied in the previous section, the father decides when the son has finished building sufficiently onto his house for his wife. The father, usually at night, finally gives permission to his son to get his bride, and the shofar (trumpet) is sounded.

Discerning the Signs of the Times

Having now established the key precept of not knowing the day nor the hour of the Rapture, let us explore or inquire further into what Christ our Lord said concerning the timing of this event.

Jesus actually scolded the Pharisees and the Sadducees (the spiritual leaders of his time) for not knowing spiritual signs of the times. Matthew 16:2-3 (NKJ): *[2] He answered and said unto them, "When it is evening, you say, 'It will be fair weather, for the sky is red'; [3] and in the morning, 'It will be foul weather today, for the sky is red and threatening.' Hypocrites! You know how to discern the face of the sky* [the earth's weather], *but you cannot **discern the signs of the times**"* [spiritual signs of a coming storm].

2 Timothy 3:1-7 describes prevailing human characteristics found on earth in the last days which we are to watch out for and veer away from: *¹ This know also, that in the **last days perilous times shall come**. ² For men shall be lovers of their own selves, covetous, boasters, proud, blasphemers, disobedient to parents, unthankful, unholy, ³ Without natural affection, trucebreakers, false accusers, incontinent, fierce, despisers of those that are good, ⁴ Traitors, heady, highminded, lovers of pleasures more than lovers of God; ⁵ Having a form of godliness, but denying the power thereof: <u>from such turn away</u>. ⁶ For of this sort are they which creep into houses, and lead captive silly women laden with sins, led away with divers lusts, ⁷ Ever learning, and never able to come to the knowledge of the truth.* Sermons could be written on each of these perilous human characteristics. Let me comment on just the last statement. Within the last 30 years of internet and cell phone inventiveness, people have almost unlimited and instant access to knowledge at their fingertips. More people go into higher education than ever before, yet polls and studies show that our people seem clueless about even a basic understanding of human knowledge and wisdom. Spiritually, they are learning fewer Biblical truths and concepts and are rejecting the Christ who said that He is *the way, the **truth,** and the life* (John 14:6a).

Luke 21:25-26: *²⁵ And there shall be...distress of nations, with perplexity...²⁶ Mens' hearts failing them for fear, and for looking after those things which are coming on the earth...* This is the only time **perplexity** is found in the New Testament. The Greek word is aporia [G640 Strong's Concordance], meaning: quandary, to have no way out. Do you feel that there is no way out of this nation's problems? Then look up, for your Redeemer draws near.

Matthew 24:3-14 and Mark 13:3-13 repeat a fairly well-known list of signs or events preceding His coming and secondly, signs of the end of the world that Jesus gave us. [Be careful not to let these two separate topics get mixed up or cause confusion.] The list of signs preceding His coming includes: many will be deceived by false Christs, wars and rumors of wars, famines, pestilences (plagues or diseases), earthquakes, much persecution of God's people, iniquity shall abound, the love of many will wax cold, the Gospel shall be preached to the entire world, and then shall the end come. At this point, Jesus goes into a description of tribulation events.

In the last century, each world war became worse. World War I killed roughly 16 million people, World War II killed 50-60 million, and the Cold War "hot spots" like Korea, Vietnam, etc. killed millions, with an estimated 100 million people killed within the 30-plus countries that were controlled by or practiced Communism.

The persecution of God's people—the Jews and Christians—has resulted in the Holocaust killing over six million Jews, and the little-reported or silent destruction of

Christianity in its heartland (starting place)—the Middle East. Here Christians were the vast majority of the population for centuries—until Islam arrived and began its Jihadist persecutions, forced conversions, and annihilations. Tens of millions of Christians have silently been killed. Experts on the matter estimate that today over 100,000 Christians die each year due to persecution. For example, the Armenian genocide alone killed one to one-and-a-half million Armenian Christians; roughly a million other Greek Orthodox, Syrian Orthodox, Assyrian and Protestant Christians in and around the Ottoman Empire (Turkey today) were also killed at the turn of the 20th Century. However, few know of it. At a two-week long conference of a large number of history teachers that I attended, I was stunned that no one except myself knew of the Armenian genocide. A television documentary about the event surprised and horrified everyone who watched it. If our teachers do not know of this event, then our children will never learn of it either. People today seem surprised to hear of the Islamic State, Boko Haram, Hezbollah, Al-Qaeda, the Taliban, Hamas, Al-Shabab, Abu Sayyaf, the Wahabi, Muslim Brotherhood, and etc. massacres of Christian groups such as: Assyrians, Nigerians, Lebanese, Coptic Egyptians, and Sudanese. They are also massacring non-Christian groups such as: Zoroastrians, Baha'i, Hindus, Buddhists, etc. For most, this seems to be a new horror, when in reality it is a continuation of historical persecution and annihilations of God's people that has been occurring for centuries. However, persecution is and will continue to get worse as we approach His coming.

These martyred saints, as well as the saints of today, and all of nature cry and groan for God's righteous justice on this earth and for His Son's quick return as described in Revelation 6:9-10 (NIV): [9] *...I saw under the altar the souls of those who had been slain because of the word of God and the testimony they had maintained.* [10] *They called out in a loud voice,* **"How long, Sovereign Lord,** *holy and true,* **until you judge** *the inhabitants of the earth and avenge our blood?"*

All of creation on the earth, which God originally created perfect, came under His judgment because of Adam's sin. Now, because of the second Adam—Christ's sacrifice for sin, all of creation groans and waits for its deliverance from this judgment during the millennial reign of Christ on earth. Romans 8:18-23 (NIV): [18] *I consider that our present sufferings are not worth comparing with the glory that will be revealed in us.* [19] *For the creation waits in eager expectation for the children of God to be revealed.* [20] *For the creation was subjected to frustration, not by its own choice, but by the will of the one who subjected it, in hope* [21] *that the creation itself will be liberated from its bondage to decay and brought into the freedom and glory of the children of God.* [22] *We know that the whole* **creation** *has been* **groaning** *as in the pains of childbirth right up to the present time.* [23] *Not only so, but we ourselves, who have the firstfruits of the Spirit,* **groan inwardly as we wait** *eagerly for our adoption to sonship, the redemption of our bodies.*

We don't know the day nor the hour of the Rapture; however, we can't bury our heads in the proverbial sand. We now know from Scripture that we are not to be ignorant of the signs of the times. Although we may become weary or even fatigued at times, we must not allow ourselves to become spiritually dull, stagnant, or complacent! On the other side of the coin, we must fight against having our consciences or spirits seared or vexed due to all the evil end-time news and events. We are to stir ourselves up as Paul told Timothy, and be **actively watching,** praying, and groaning in anticipation of this imminent great event. If Christ scolded the spiritual leaders back in His time for not discerning the signs of the times, nor being prepared for His first historic visitation to the earth, then the same holds true for us today. We today are so near the time of His next visitation to earth!

Understanding the Fig Tree Parable—Israel

What are some other key signs or related Scriptural concepts that we need to be aware of in our spiritual watch that we can glean from Jesus as we continue on in Matthew 24:32-34/Mark 13:28-30? Jesus gave us this important but little understood parable concerning a last day's sign of His coming.

Matthew 24:32-34 (NKJ): *32 Now learn this parable from the **fig** tree: When its branch has already become tender and puts forth leaves, you know that summer is near. 33 So you* *also, when you see all these things, know that it is near, at the very doors. ^{34} Assuredly, I say to you, this generation will by no means pass away till all these things are fulfilled.*

As with many parables, in order to comprehend their meaning, we need God's further understanding of the obscure culture of that time, and it helps to do a comparative word search in a concordance. In the latter case, a concordance study of all the fig tree references in Scripture will lead us, I believe, to the conclusion that it is symbolic of the State of Israel. For example, when reading Jeremiah 24, one finds that the whole chapter is about the good and evil **figs** which represent two different groups of Jews. It says that one group would not prosper, but that God blesses the other Jewish group and they become His heart-filled people.

See if you can't perceive some similarities in the fig tree parable to that referenced in Song of Solomon, Chapter 2. Some of the wording compares to Jesus' words in Matthew 24:32-34 which we just read, as well as the Eastern wedding customs we already discussed.

Song of Solomon 2:4, 10, 13: *^{4} He brought me to the banqueting house, and his banner over me was love. ^{10} My beloved spake and said unto me, <u>Rise up</u>, my love, my fair one, and come away. ^{13}* [When] *The **fig** tree putteth forth her green figs, and the vines with the tender grapes give a good smell. <u>Arise</u>, my love, my fair one, and **come away**.*

As a miraculous sign to the world, and in preparation for His Second Coming and His reign on earth, God created the modern State of Israel *that they may see and know, and consider, and understand together, that the hand of the Lord has done this, and the Holy One of Israel has created it* (Isaiah 41:20-NKJ). After almost 2,000 years, the State of Israel was recreated in 1948; it is a place where God will prove Himself to the world through modern miracles of deliverance. The Rapture could only occur after Israel (the fig tree sign of His coming) was miraculously reestablished. That is why some Biblical scholars predicted and later became so excited when the modern State of Israel was established. That is also why so many prophecy-believing Christians are so supportive of Israel today. It is also why so much satanic, and therefore worldly, pressure is focused on trying to defame and destroy tiny Israel. It's why it is in the news every day; by modern TV, all the world *may see, and know, and consider, and understand.* As many as half a dozen different Arab nations attacked Israel and tried to destroy that fledgling nation by war in 1948, 1956, 1967, 1973, etc. No matter in what year this book is read, I'm sure that furious warfare against Israel will be occurring.

Satan hates God and all of God's creation—especially the Jews and the Church to whom God's covenant promises and blessings are given. God cannot fulfill hundreds of end-time prophecies if Israel doesn't exist; Israel is in the epicenter of a huge spiritual struggle, which the Bible is clear that

God wins in the end! In the meantime, the focus of the whole world is now on the Middle East, especially on the tiny nation of Israel (again, only about the size of New Jersey or about one-tenth the size of my state of Colorado). The conflicts in and over this Mid-East area constantly boil over to involve the rest of the world. God is focusing world attention on the area and nation that He is doing miraculous things through. This turmoil will continue until Jesus returns, and He—the world's King of Kings—sets up His earthly kingdom and His capital in Jerusalem. For further diligent study: Psalm 87, Zechariah 1:14, 2 Kings 21:7, Ezekiel 5:5, Psalm 76:2, Matthew 5:34-35, Joel 3:1-2, 16-17, Zechariah 12:1-10, Zechariah 14:2-4, 9, 16-17, Jeremiah 23:5-6, Jeremiah 3:17, Isaiah 24:23, Isaiah 2:1-3, Micah 4:2, Hebrews 12:22-23, Revelation 20:7-9.

We dare not fight against what God is doing. Read the following end-times Scripture and then decide if you want to oppose God or mess with His heritage Israel. Isaiah 41:8-20 (NKJ): *⁸ But you, Israel, are My servant, Jacob, whom I have chosen, The descendants of Abraham My friend. ⁹ You whom I have taken from the **ends of the earth,** And called from **its farthest regions,** And said to You, You are My servant; I have chosen you and have not cast you away: ¹⁰ Fear not, for I am with you; Be not dismayed, for I am your God. I will strengthen you, Yes, I will help you, I will uphold you with My righteous right hand. ¹¹ Behold, all those who were incensed against you Shall be ashamed and disgraced; They* *shall be as nothing, And those who strive with you shall per-ish.* [12] *...Those who war against you Shall be as nothing, As a nonexistent thing.* [13] *For I, the Lord your God, will hold your right hand, Saying to you, 'Fear not, I will help you.'* [14] *"Fear not, you worm Jacob, You men of Israel! I will help you," says the Lord And your Redeemer, the Holy One of Israel.* [15] *Behold, I will make you into a new threshing sledge with sharp teeth...* [17b] *...I, the Lord, will hear them; I, the God of Israel, will not forsake them...* [20] *That they* **may see and know, And consider and understand** *together, That the hand of the* **Lord has done this, And the Holy One of Israel has created it.**

We know this is an end-times prophecy because of verse nine. Ancient Israel was called out of just one nation—Egypt. Later, they were again regathered from one nation—Babylon (Persia), but never from the *ends of the earth* or from *its farthest regions* until the modern-day regathering of Israel. The next Scripture below is also a last day's prophecy as it says that Israel will be gathered from *all nations.*

Joel 3:1-2 (NKJ): [1] *"...When I bring back the captives of Judah and Jerusalem,* [2] *I will also gather all nations, And bring them down to the valley of Jehoshaphat* (decision, judgment); *And I will enter into judgment with them there On account of* **My people, My heritage Israel,** *Whom they have scattered among the nations. They have also divided up* **My land.***"*

Israel is God's people, heritage and land (Genesis 15:18, 17:8, Deuteronomy 7:6-8, 32:8-10, Jeremiah 27:5, Zechariah 2:12). Yet today people and nations are *incensed against, strive against, war against, plot and conspire against, to destroy* this tiny nation like no other on earth in all of history (Isaiah 41:11-12, Psalm 83:3-4). Why is this? It has to be a satanic battle. The world (UN) dares not tell any other nation where they can't build homes or declare their capital. They are also trying to divide tiny Israel and take away key Jewish areas such as historical Judea and Samaria (the so-called West Bank). The land modern-day Jordan occupies was originally promised to Israel by Great Britain, but it was split off to be a homeland for Palestinians (which makes up two-thirds of Jordan's population) just before Israel was created in 1948. Israel has given the Sinai Peninsula (over twice the size of Israel today) to Egypt several times for a promise of land for peace. Obviously this did not work the first time, and now terrorist groups (including ISIS) occupy much of the Sinai as a base to attack Israel. Hoping to appease the world and her enemies, Israel also pulled out of Southern Lebanon and the Gaza Strip only to have them occupied by terrorist groups like Hezbollah and Hamas, who are determined to destroy Israel today with tens of thousands of rockets and missiles. What a dangerous neighborhood Israel lives in. Still many call for Israel to give up more PIECES of land, which would reduce it to a width of as little as ten miles, for the elusive and deceptive promise of PEACE from those who won't even recognize Israel's right to exist and who openly scream daily that their goal is to destroy Israel and take what's left of her land. Appeasement or capitulation—PIECES for PEACE—has never worked historically; it only encourages your enemy to demand more. As David sorrowfully and regretfully opined in Psalm 120:7: *I am for peace: but when I speak, they are for war.*

This is to become our prayer. Psalm 83:1-4 (NIV): *[1] O God, do not remain silent; do not turn a deaf ear, do not stand aloof, O God. [2] See how your enemies growl, how your foes rear their heads. [3] With cunning they conspire against your people; they plot against those you cherish. [4] "Come," they say, "let us destroy them as a nation, so that Israel's name is remembered no more."*

Believers are to search the Scriptures, unify with God's heart, and support what God is doing in and through Israel. How can I say that? Psalm 102:13 and 16 say: *[13] Thou shall arise, and have mercy upon Zion* [Jerusalem/Israel]: *for the time to favour her, yea the set time, is come. [16] **When the Lord shall build up Zion*** [which He is doing now again], ***he shall appear in his glory.*** Psalm 122:6: *Pray for the peace of Jerusalem: they shall prosper that love thee.*

You may be wondering why this section on the Parable of the Fig Tree—Israel is longer and more detailed than previous sections. Israel is God's visible sign and time clock to the world. Unlike most subtopics about **"When,"** it is a controversial topic within the Church today as well as the world. This book makes a clear stand and statement on this issue.

Let's elaborate a bit more on why Israel plays such a big part in end-time prophecy. God has planned so much more for the Church and His Jewish brethren. What plans and blessings He has in store for both.

We discover from Ephesians Chapters 2 and 3 that it is in God's plan that the faithful Church and faithful Israel will be united before God in the future. Ephesians 2:11 talks about the uncircumcised Gentile believers and the circumcised faithful believing Jews. Ephesians 2:12 then speaks about those Gentiles, who were once aliens and strangers, now being united into the **Commonwealth of Israel.** Like the British Commonwealth, some people in areas around the world share a similar culture, language, religion, law system, type of government, etc. These have a wealth of culture in common. Ephesians 2:13-16a: [13] *But now in Christ Jesus ye who sometimes were far off are made nigh by the blood of Christ.* [14] *For he is our peace, who hath made **both one**...* [15] *...for to make in himself of **twain one new man**, so making peace.* [16a] *And that he might **reconcile both** unto God in **one body** by the cross...* The Living Bible makes comments like: *...making us all one family...he fused us together to become one new person...both of us reconciled unto God.* At God's wedding feast—the marriage of the Lamb—both families of faith will be bonded to each other and united as one by marriage.

Romans 3:29-30 states: [29] *Is he the God of the Jews only? Is he not also of the Gentiles? Yes, of the Gentiles also:* [30] *Seeing it is one God, which shall justify the circumcision by faith, and uncircumcision through faith.*

Ephesians 2:19-20 adds: [19] *Now therefore ye are no more strangers and foreigners, but **fellowcitizens** with the saints, and of the household of God;* [20] *And are built upon the foundation of the apostles* [New Testament] *and prophets* [Old Testament], *Jesus Christ himself being the chief cornerstone;* In Ephesians 3:9, Paul called this the ***fellowship of the mystery.*** J.R.R. Tolkien, a famous Christian author, may have drawn his analogy of the "fellowship of the ring" from these Scriptures.

Ruth, in the book of the Bible that bears her name, foreshadowed what God was going to do in the spiritual realm of unity between Jews and Gentile believers. Born a Gentile, she married a Jewish man. Either disgust for her own culture or religion and/or a newly gained respect for Judaism, which she gained from her in-laws, caused a great change in Ruth. Upon her husband's death, she joined herself to her mother-in-law Naomi, and she refused to remain in her old country and culture when Naomi decided to return to Israel. Unlike Lot's wife, she refused to look back to the old, but pressed forward with Naomi into a new culture and religion. She said in Ruth 1:16b (NKJ): ... *Your people shall be my people, And your God, my God.* In the end, she came to Bethlehem, married Boaz, and became part of the lineage of David and later of Jesus. She was no longer a stranger or foreigner, but a **fellowcitizen** of the **Commonwealth of Israel** and the household of God.

I believe that the previous Scriptures and dozens more on the faithfulness of God to keep His covenant promises to Abraham and the Jewish people prove that God is **not** a God of replacement theology or supersessionism—the belief that God is finished with the Jews and gave all their covenant promises to the Church. I believe that God is not into what I call subtraction theology, but that He is into positive addition theology.

The whole chapter of Romans 11 is clear on this matter. Romans 11:1a (Living) asks and then answers itself: ...*has God rejected and deserted his people the Jews? Oh no, not at all...* Romans 11:17-27 (NIV) states: *[17] If **some** of the branches have been broken off, and you* [Gentiles/Church], *though a wild olive shoot, have been grafted in among the others and now share in the nourishing sap from the olive root, [18] do not consider yourself to be superior to those other branches. If you do, consider this: You do not support the root, but the root supports you. [But you must be careful **not to** brag about being put into **replace** (replacement theology) the branches that were broken off—Living] [19] You will say then, "Branches were broken off so that I could be grafted in." [20] Granted. But they were broken off because of unbelief, and you stand by faith. Do not be arrogant, but tremble. [21] For if God did not spare the natural branches, he will not spare you either. [22] Consider therefore the kindness and sternness of*

*God: sternness to those who fell, but kindness to you, provided that you continue in his kindness. Otherwise, you also will be cut off. [23] And if they do not persist in unbelief, they will be grafted in, for **God is able to graft them in again.** [24] After all, if you were cut out of an olive tree that is wild by nature, and contrary to nature were grafted into a cultivated olive tree, how much more readily will these, the natural branches, be grafted into their own olive tree! [25] I do not want you to be ignorant of this **mystery,** brothers and sisters, so that you may not be conceited: Israel has experienced a hardening in part until the full number of the Gentiles has come in, [26] and in this way **all Israel will be saved.** As it is written: "The deliverer will come from Zion; he will turn godlessness away from Jacob. [27] And this is **my covenant** with them when I take away their sins."* At the end of the tribulation—entering into the millennial reign of Christ on earth—...*all Israel shall be saved*...(verse 26) Why? The answer is found in verse 27: *For this is my covenant with them...!* Paul confirms that His covenant is an **everlasting covenant**.

Many Scriptures make it clear that His covenant with the Jews is an everlasting one, and cannot be annulled or replaced by anyone, even the Church. For example, Psalm 105:8-11 (RSV) says: [8] *He is **mindful of his covenant for ever,** of the word that he commanded, **for a thousand generations,** [9] the covenant which he made with Abraham, his sworn promise to Isaac, [10] which he confirmed to Jacob as a statute, to Israel as an **everlasting covenant,** [11] saying, "To* *you I will give the land of Canaan as your portion for an inheritance."*

Isaiah 54:5-10 says: ⁵ *For **thy Maker is thine husband**... the Holy One of **Israel**... ⁷ For a small moment have I forsaken thee; but with great mercies will I gather thee. ⁸ In a little wrath I hid my face from thee for a moment; but with **everlasting kindness** will I have mercy on thee, saith the Lord thy Redeemer... ¹⁰ For the mountains shall depart, and the hills be removed; but **my kindness shall not depart from thee, neither shall the covenant of my peace be removed, saith the Lord that hath mercy on thee.***

Isaiah 66:22 says: *For as the new heavens and the new earth, which I will make, shall remain before me, saith the Lord, so shall your seed and your name remain.* (Israel and Jerusalem are named in verse 20.) Israel will continue to exist in the new heavens and the new earth that God will create in the future. Another book would be required to cover this topic, but I will give a few more references concerning God's everlasting covenant to Israel for the diligent to study on your own: Jeremiah 32:37, 40 and 42; Ezekiel 37:26; Genesis 17:7-8; Jeremiah 31:35-37; Jeremiah 33:24-26; Jeremiah 46:28; Psalm 89:3-4, 30-37; Isaiah 49:13-16; and Malachi 3:6.

As In the Evil Days of Noah

Our key chapter, Matthew 24, continues into the next sign or principle. Verse 36 again states the basic rule concerning not knowing the exact timing of the Rapture, but then adds a sign that we have to further understand and take deeply into our modern man's spirit. Noah is especially important for us to more fully comprehend, because the modern days in which we find ourselves today are similar to that of Noah's time.

In Matthew 24:36-39, Jesus said: *[36] But of that day and hour knoweth no man, no, not the angels of heaven, but my Father only. [37] But as the days of Noe (Noah) were, so shall also the coming of the Son of man be. [38] For as in the days that were before the flood they were eating and drinking, marrying and giving in marriage, until the day that Noe (Noah) entered into the ark, [39] And knew not until the flood came, and took them all away; so shall also the coming of the Son of man be.*

Eating, drinking, and marriage aren't bad or harmful—are they? No, unless all we do is feed our flesh and put all the cares of this life at a higher level of importance before our spiritual walk with God. Man has a body, soul and spirit. God wants our spirit life to thrive. Martha and Mary, both close friends of Jesus, are our examples. Luke 10:38-42 (Living): *[38] As Jesus and the disciples continued on their way to Jerusalem they came to a village where a woman named Martha welcomed them into her home. [39] Her sister Mary sat on the floor, <u>listening to Jesus</u> as he talked. [40] But Martha was the jittery [anxious] type, and was worrying over the big dinner she was preparing. She came to Jesus* *and said, "Sir, doesn't it seem unfair to you that my sister just sits here while I do all the work? Tell her to come and help me." ⁴¹But the Lord said to her, "Martha, dear friend, you are so upset over all these details! ⁴² There is really **only one thing worth being concerned about**. Mary has discovered it—and I won't take it away from her!"*

After forty days of fasting, Jesus was tempted by Satan to turn stones into bread and feed himself. *But he (Jesus) answered and said, "It is written, Man shall not live by bread alone, but by every word that proceedeth out of the mouth of God"* (Matthew 4:4). Jesus was teaching us what should be the key priority in life. Feeding our fleshly desires must be put into subordination to the things of God, which was not the case in the days of Noah.

What else was the evil like in the days of Noah that brought such a complete judgment and destruction to the earth? We must go back to find out what was so evil or wrong with mankind as they carried out their basic life functions. The answer is found in Genesis 6:3a, 5-7 (NIV): *³ Then the LORD said, "My Spirit will not contend with humans forever, for they are mortal"... ⁵ The LORD saw how great the wickedness of the human race had become on the earth, and that every inclination of the thoughts of the human heart was only evil all the time. ⁶ The LORD regretted that he had made human beings on the earth, and his heart was deeply troubled. ⁷ So the LORD said, "I will wipe from the face of the earth the human race I have created"...*

Not only did they not put God first in their hearts and lives, but they were exceedingly wicked, and God knew every thought, imagination, and fantasy of their heart was evil continually. In our present time, I fear that we are just like it was in the days of Noah; we are so harried or vexed that we may not even realize it. We, too, should comprehend that judgment is coming to this earth, and we believers should live accordingly. Like Noah, we are to prepare our spiritual ark of safety—prepare for the Rapture before the coming judgment or tribulation of God.

Let's examine some of the characteristics that caused grace to come to Noah and his family. Genesis 6:8-9, 22: *8 But Noah found grace in the eyes of the Lord. 9 ...Noah was a just man and perfect in his generations, and Noah walked with God. 22 Thus did Noah; according to all that God commanded him, so did he.* Hebrews 11:7 says: ***By faith*** *Noah, being warned of God of things not seen as yet, **moved with fear** [the awe, reverence, or healthy fear of the Lord], **prepared** an ark to the saving of his house; by the which he condemned the world, and became heir of the righteousness which is **by faith.***

Noah believed God concerning the coming unprecedented judgment or tribulation. He had faith in the Word of God, and he heartily prepared to escape the coming judgment of God by building the ark. He kept his eyes on God and the heavens. He had to ignore many of life's normal demands and the people's criticism and mockery. The Hebrew word for "ark" is "box"; a box is like a coffin. In a sense, Noah died to himself and this normal life on earth, so that he could live eternally. Saving his family and the animal kingdoms was all that occupied his time and energy. Among all the people on earth, he and only a few of his family were saved from the severe judgment of God for that time period. What a challenge and example he is to us. We are to be as single-minded and as faithful as Noah was.

Matthew 24:37 reminds us: *But* **as the days of Noe (Noah) were,** *so shall also the coming of the Son of man be.* God has now warned us that our era is extremely evil. Can we see it, or are we, like Lot, so vexed by the magnitude of the depravity and wickedness around us, that our consciences have become seared and hardened? Our era will end in severe tribulation and the judgment of God, even as Noah's era ended with the flood judgment. The rain/flood judgment of Noah's time was unlike anything ever seen before; they had never even seen rain before, only dew. The Great Tribulation judgment will also be totally unique and unlike anything man can imagine [Revelation 6-18]. The belief that judgment was coming was rejected by the people of Noah's time and is being rejected by most people of our era today. However, if we believe in this coming judgment and means of escape (the Rapture), we will live differently from all those around us, and we will prepare accordingly.

Like it was in Noah's time, when God's justice and love supernaturally prepared Noah to save him from that earthly judgment to come, God is lovingly calling the Church today to prepare to meet Him before the coming tribulation. What lifestyle changes and work was involved in preparing for the flood by Noah and his family? What lifestyle changes and work is God requiring of us in preparation for the Rapture?

When the time came, Scripture says that God closed the door of Noah's ark. Similarly, He will carry us safely to Heaven while this earth suffers horrible tribulation and death.

Many Were Not Ready, Nor Taken

To glean another Rapture principle, or sign of the times, let's again read further in our key chapter, Matthew 24, this time reading verses 40-41: *[40] Then shall two be in the field; the one shall be taken, and the other left. [41] Two women shall be grinding at the mill; the one shall be taken, and the other left.*

Later we will study the parable of the ten virgins (Matthew 25:1-13); in this parable, only five out of the ten virgins had oil in their lamps and were ready and made it into heaven for the marriage to the Bridegroom. Lack of readiness will be a problem in the last days. Christ, our Bridegroom, will come for us, His Bride, when least expected.

Notice here that half of the persons mentioned are taken or raptured. Does this mean half of the world's population?

No, it can't mean that. Half of the world's population doesn't even claim any faith in Christianity; cultural Christianity today is roughly one-fifth to one-fourth of the world's population. If not half of the world's population, then half of what group is Christ talking about? More on this later, but it is a teaser for now of things to come in this book.

Let's continue even further in Matthew 24 (verses 42-51). Many title this parable as The Parable of the Two Servants because it is talking about servants or believers of our Lord. It is not about one being a believer and another being an unbeliever. It also begins with our basic Rapture precept: *[42]* **_Watch_** *therefore: for ye know not what hour your Lord doth come. [43] But know this, that if the goodman of the house had known in what **watch** the **thief** would come, he would have **watched**, and would not have suffered his house to be broken up. [44] Therefore **be** ye also **ready**: for in such an hour as ye think not the Son of man cometh. [45] Who then is a **faithful** and **wise servant**, whom his lord hath made ruler over his household, to give them meat in due season? [46] Blessed is that servant, whom his lord when he cometh shall find so **doing**. [47] Verily I say unto you, That he shall make him ruler over all his goods. [48] But and if that evil servant shall say in his heart, My lord **delayeth his coming;** [49] And shall begin to smite his fellowservants, and to eat and drink with the drunken; [50] The lord of that servant shall come in a day when he **looketh not** for him, and in an hour that he is **not aware** of, [51] And shall cut him asunder, and appoint him his portion with the hypocrites: there shall be weeping and gnashing of teeth.*

Notice that we have seen the command to **watch** four times before in Mark 13:32-37, and now three more times in this latest passage. We will also see it much more in the future. It is the key word or command to us concerning the Rapture. It is the foremost characteristic of the **"Who"** or of the person who will be raptured.

Also notice more of the underlined **"Who"** characteristics; Jesus, through Matthew, implores us to be faithful, watchful, wise, and hard-working servants of God. We must avoid the fallen servant's unfaithful attitude and behavior, which partially results from the delay in the coming of his Master. If this unfaithful servant had understood and taken seriously the Scriptures concerning the reason for the delay, which we will explore next, maybe he or she would have persevered.

The Father Delays His Son's Coming—Why?

There are two concepts that need to be expounded on further from the previous Matthew 24:42-51 text. One is the statement that: *...my Lord delays his coming,* and the second is the "thief in the night" idea. First we will ponder the delay and why it occurs.

Matthew 25:5 & 19: *⁵ While the **bridegroom tarried**, they all slumbered and slept: ¹⁹ After a **long time** the lord of those servants cometh, and reckoneth with them.*

Scripture, I believe, actually explains to us why the Father delays His Son's coming to get His Bride. This is important and heartening for us to know; at least we can understand and appreciate the reason why.

James 5:7-8, 9b: *⁷ Be patient therefore, brethren, unto the coming of the Lord. Behold, the **husbandman waiteth** for the precious fruit of the earth, and hath <u>long patience</u> for it, until he receive the early and latter rain. ⁸ <u>Be ye also patient; stablish your hearts:</u> for the coming of the Lord draweth nigh. ⁹ᵇ ...behold, the judge standeth before the door.* "Stablish," which in the Greek is sterizo [4741 Strong's Concordance], means to: turn resolutely in a certain direction, make steadfast, and/or strengthen. Notice Christ the Judge stands ready to judge the Church for rewards at His [bema] judgment seat and to open the seals of judgment upon this world at the start of the tribulation [Revelation 6].

Our loving Father is waiting for the full harvest of souls around the world. This should be encouraging and reassuring to us as we look on the bright side of a seemingly negative delay. It is helpful to know the reason for the delay, but we need patience and perseverance to overcome as things get worse in our nation and the world. It seems that the reason the Father has delayed Jesus' return is because there is to be a latter rain—a last day harvest that must be brought in before spiritual winter arrives. Near the end of this book, the Parable of the Excuses found in Luke 14:16-24 gives even further insight into the Father's desire to have His Kingdom full with his faithful people. The Scriptural hints of a delay or tarrying of Christ's return indicate that the Church has not fulfilled its Great Commission as of yet, and that we are behind schedule.

Matthew 9:37-38 (NKJ): *[37] Then He said to His disciples, "The harvest truly is plentiful, but the laborers are few. [38] Therefore pray the Lord of the harvest to send out laborers into His harvest."* If the Church really wants Christ our Bridegroom to return, then we should be busy doing our Great Commission duty in helping to take God's Word to every area of the world. God, in His great love and mercy, does not want any area of the world or anyone to be left out of His Kingdom. If we are getting impatient, then we really need to be working harder at the Kingdom's work; don't be like the unfaithful servant in Matthew 24. The James 5 passage tells us to be patient, just like God is longsuffering and patient in waiting for the final harvest. Remember that the last item in the list of signs that Jesus gave His disciples in Matthew 24:14 was: *And this <u>gospel</u> of the kingdom shall be <u>preached in all the world</u> for a witness unto all nations; and* [only] *then shall the end come.*

There are also Scriptures that point to a latter day falling away (2 Thessalonians 2:3) at the same time as God's latter day outpouring, revival, and harvest. How is this supposed contradiction possible? The rush of life and materialism are great problems of the so-called Christian world today, especially in the United States and Europe. God foresaw it and warned us so that we should fight against materialism and covetousness in our lives. We must also fight the fight of faith continually against any and all evil imaginations in our thought life; this was God's condemnation of Noah's era, and is the modern day mirror image of our end times era.

In Mark 4:19 and Matthew 13:22, Jesus spoke about how the cares of the world and the deceitfulness of riches are like thorns, thistles, and weeds that will easily choke the Word and the spiritual life out of us if we are not careful. Weeds take consistent and continuous effort to keep out of our yards, gardens, or fields. We can never let down. We are to love God with all of our heart, mind, and strength; it's only right for Him to assess our love for Him in the daily choices that we make.

Again, in the Luke 14 Parable of the Excuses, which we will study in depth near the end of the book, you will find that when the wedding supper was ready, and the people were called to come, they all made light of it and made worldly excuses (family, jobs, and riches) as to why they could not attend. They missed out. God then **delayed** the supper. Let me repeat. He **delayed** the much-anticipated wedding feast of our Lord Jesus, while He searched the byways of the world to fill His Son's wedding feast. Let us not be one of those who make excuses; let us always put God first. While many fall away in so-called "Christian" Europe and the United States, God, at the same time, is pouring out a great revival in Africa and Asia and the byways of this world. Most of this goes unreported by our secular media. Why? First, it does a horrible job of reporting on most Third World areas of the earth in its news. Second, it is not sympathetic to report any positive news about Christianity due to its secular bias. Third, good news seldom makes it into the news anyway.

While the **delay** causes doubters and scoffers to arise, it also creates a refining and purifying separation, according to God's purposes.

2 Peter 3:3-4, 8-10a, (NKJ): *³ knowing this first: that scoffers* [G1703 Strong's Concordance—empaiktes—meaning mockers, false teachers] *will come in the last days, walking according to their own lusts, ⁴ and saying, "Where is the promise of His coming? For since the fathers fell asleep, all things continue as they were from the beginning of creation." ⁸ But, beloved, do not forget this one thing, that with the Lord one day is as a thousand years, and a thousand years as one day. ⁹ The Lord is not slack* (slow) *concerning His promise, as some count slackness, but is longsuffering toward us, not willing that any should perish but that all should come to repentance. ¹⁰ᵃ But the day of the Lord will come as a* **thief in the night.**

Let's summarize several concepts here for emphasis. First, doubt about the Rapture will even come from members of the Church in the end times, especially worldly members *"walking according to their own lusts."* After all, if there isn't an imminent coming of our Lord, then we can just continue living normal lives in the pursuit of this world and its many distractions and lusts. Second, the delay allows more to be saved and gathered into the kingdom; God doesn't want any to perish. Third, the delay causes a refining separation even within the Church—a sheep and goats type of separation or judgment [Matthew 25:31-46]. Fourth, in the Rapture, Christ comes as a **thief in the night.** What should we do with these truths? The next verse tells us:

2 Peter 3:11b (NKJ): *...what manner of persons ought you to be in holy conduct and godliness?* This is the famous Francis Schaeffer question: "**What manner of persons ought we to be?**" This again gets more into the characteristics or qualities of the "**Who**" part of our study, as do verses 14-17 of 2 Peter 3 which go on to command us <u>to be holy,</u> <u>looking for that day,</u> <u>diligent,</u> <u>without spot or wrinkle,</u> <u>blameless,</u> and finally, to <u>beware lest we fall from our steadfastness.</u>

As I organized, wrote, and struggled over the content of this book, many verses and concepts were added by the Lord in many different ways over the two-to-three year process. One night, this obscure verse kept coming to me over and over in my sleep. Luke 18:8b: *...when the Son of man cometh, shall he find faith on the earth?* The next morning, I looked up its reference and read the chapter. At first, the verse seemed to be unrelated to the Parable of the Woman and the Judge or what I now call the Parable of Perseverance, found in Luke 18:1-8:

¹ And he spake a parable unto them to this end, that men ought always to <u>pray</u>, and <u>not to faint</u>; ² Saying, There was in a city a judge, which feared not God, neither regarded man: ³ And there was a widow in that city; and she came unto him, saying, Avenge me of mine adversary. ⁴ And he would not for a while: but afterward he said within himself, Though I fear not God, nor regard man; ⁵ Yet because this widow troubleth me, I will avenge her, lest by her continual coming she weary me. ⁶ And the Lord said, Hear what the unjust judge saith. ⁷ And shall not God avenge his own elect, which cry day and night unto him, though he bear long with them? ⁸ I tell you that he will avenge them speedily. Nevertheless when the Son of man cometh, shall he find faith on the earth?

The theme of this parable is obviously persistence or perseverance, just like the Parable of the Persistent Friend in Luke 11:5-13. The last half of verse eight seems to be saying that in the last days before His coming, there will be tough days when many things will be delayed, including answers to prayer. Our faith will be tested, and we will have to persevere in our faith. Even though there is a delay in His coming, this must not destroy our faith. We will have to hold fast, stand firm, and be diligent in our faith toward God.

The "Thief in the Night" Scenario

The second concept learned from Matthew 24:43 is the idea of Christ being the "thief in the night." Christ as a thief?! What does the Creator of all of the universe need to steal? What does He mean by this statement? Christ will steal away His Bride in dark times. It will be sudden, unexpected, and it will be devastating to those left behind. Paul also uses the phrase "thief in the night" in 1 Thessalonians 5:1-23: *¹ But of the times and the seasons, brethren, ye have no need that I write unto you. ² For yourselves know perfectly that the day of the Lord so cometh as a **thief in the night**. ³ For when they shall say, Peace and safety; then **sudden destruction cometh** upon them, as travail upon a woman with child; and they shall not escape.*

Let me make two comments about verse 3 above before proceeding further into the text. First, with a pregnant woman, the signs are there (swollen stomach, etc.); the general time or month she knows, but she doesn't know the exact day or hour of her delivery. Second, Luke 21:35 likens this *sudden destruction* as unto a snare or a trap snapping shut. If destruction is coming as verse 3 says, then it has to be at the beginning of the tribulation, not mid- or post-tribulation when they would already have experienced massive worldwide destruction with over half of the population of the world destroyed.

*⁴ But ye, brethren, are not in darkness, that that day should overtake you as a **thief**. ⁵ Ye are all the children of light, and the children of the day: we are not of the night, nor of darkness. ⁶ Therefore let us <u>not sleep</u>, as do others; but let us <u>**watch**</u> and <u>be sober</u>. ⁷ For they that sleep sleep in the night; and they that be drunken are drunken in the night. ⁸ But let us, who are of the day, <u>be sober</u>, putting on the breastplate* of *faith and love*; and for an helmet, the *hope* of salvation. *⁹ For God hath not appointed us to wrath* [tribulation], *but to obtain salvation by our Lord Jesus Christ,* *¹⁰ Who died for us, that, whether we wake* [the living are raptured] *or sleep* [the dead are resurrected], *we should live together with him.* *¹¹ Wherefore comfort yourselves together, and edify one another, even as also ye do.*

We are again told to *comfort ourselves together.* Do you recall the Greek meaning of this word "comfort" that we studied in 1 Thessalonians 4:16-18, the very first Scriptural reference of this book? Again, it means to invite, implore, invoke, exhort, entreat, beseech, and/or call near.

Paul continues on in verses 12-23 of 1 Thessalonians 5 to beseech believers as to how true Christians should live and respond to this "thief in the night" scenario and time period. It again points to the characteristics of the **"Who"** or those that are raptured. *¹² And we beseech you, brethren, to know them which labour among you, and are over you in the Lord, and admonish you;* *¹³ And to esteem them very highly in love for their work's sake. And be at peace among yourselves.* *¹⁴ Now we exhort you, brethren, warn them that are unruly, comfort the feebleminded, support the weak, be patient toward all men.* *¹⁵ See that none render evil for evil unto any man; but ever follow that which is good, both among yourselves, and to all men.* *¹⁶ Rejoice evermore.* *¹⁷ Pray without ceasing.* *¹⁸ In every thing give thanks: for this is the will of God in Christ Jesus concerning you.* *¹⁹ Quench not the*

Spirit. [20] *Despise not prophesyings.* [21] *Prove all things; hold fast that which is good.* [22] *Abstain from all appearance of evil.* [23] *And the very God of peace sanctify you wholly; and I pray God your whole spirit and soul and body* **be preserved blameless unto the coming of our Lord Jesus Christ.**

What a list! What a challenge for us!

To the church of Sardis, the command in Revelation 3:2-3 was: [2] *Be* **watchful,** *and strengthen the things which remain, that are ready to die: for I have not found thy works perfect before God.* [3] *Remember therefore how thou hast received and heard, and* <u>hold fast</u>, *and* <u>repent</u>. *If therefore thou shalt not* **watch,** *I will come on thee as a thief* [in the night], *and thou shalt not know what hour I will come upon thee.*

In the Rapture, Christ comes unseen by the world, in the twinkling of an eye, as a **thief in the night,** a thief coming to steal His Bride away in dark times when least expected. This is quite different than when He comes seven years later at His Second Coming at the end of the Great Tribulation. Then He comes as the King of Kings **with** His Bride after the Marriage Supper of the Lamb. At His Second Coming, all men will see Him. Rev. 1:7 (NIV): *"Look, he is coming with the clouds,"* and *"every eye will see him, even those who pierced him"* [Zechariah 12:8-11 and 13:6]; *and all peoples on the earth "will mourn because of him." So shall it be! Amen.* (They mourn because of their earlier rejection of Him and because of all of the suffering and death that it caused over centuries of time.)

At His Revelation or Second Coming at the end of the tribulation, Christ—the King of Kings—leaves heaven on a white horse, followed by armies also on white horses which have already been in heaven. Christ will fight the Anti-Christ and his armies and prevail (Revelation 19:11-21). 1 Thessalonians 3:13b says that ...*the coming of our Lord Jesus Christ* is **with** *all of his saints.* Jude 1:14b-15a explains: [14b]...*behold, the Lord cometh* **with** *ten thousands of his saints,* [15a] *To execute judgment upon all, and to convince all that are ungodly among them of all their ungodly deeds...* Colossians 3:4 states that: *When Christ, who is our life, shall appear, then shall ye also appear* **with** *him in glory.* Christ can't be coming for the Church at the end of the seven years of Great Tribulation if He's coming **with** the Church.

Let's highlight key ideas in Zechariah Chapter 14: [1] *Behold the day of the Lord cometh...* [2] *All nations* [come] *against Jerusalem to battle... half of the city shall go forth into captivity...* [3] *the Lord will fight against those nations...* [4] *His feet will stand upon the Mount of Olives... and it will cleave in the midst...* [5] *...and the Lord my God shall come and all the saints* **with** *thee.* [9] *The Lord shall be king over all the earth.* Joel Chapters 2 and 3, Isaiah Chapter 13, 30:26-28, 34:1-8, and 63:1-9 are further reference examples concerning His Second Coming. As we can see, all these Scriptures about the Second Coming are totally different in nature from the **thief in the night**—Rapture scenario.

Before the Anti-Christ Can Be Revealed

Since the fall of Adam and Eve, life on earth for mankind is fraught with many troubles, problems, and trials.

John 16:33 (NKJ): *...In the world, you will have tribulation.*

In the original Greek text, tribulation [G2346 and G2347 Strong's Concordance] means: burdens, trials, afflictions, trouble, persecution, anguish. Sooner or later, trials or tribulation will come in some fashion into everyone's life. It is also normal for more tribulation and persecution to come into the life of a person who is a Christian and is living according to God's Word (Matthew 13:21). Some believers in the world, however, must endure much tribulation to enter into the Kingdom of God (Acts 14:22). Some trials and tribulations are caused by Satan's attacks on our lives, and unfortunately, some are the natural consequences of our own mistakes and our poor lifestyle choices. We are told, however, that in the midst of tribulations or problems in life, that we are to be patient (Romans 12:12), even to be joyful (2 Corinthians 7:4), and that we are to be persuaded that neither normal tribulations nor any other thing can be allowed to separate us from God (Romans 8:35-39).

In our key chapter of Matthew 24, verse 21 says, however: *For then shall be **great tribulation,** such as was not since the beginning of the world to this time, no, nor ever shall be.*

A study on the Great Tribulation Scriptures would also be another whole separate book and it can only be briefly summarized here. The Great Tribulation is much different from normal tribulations or even special times of trouble in life. As in the time of Noah's flood, Sodom and Gomorrah's destruction, the plagues of Pharaoh's Egypt, etc., this is God's judgment on the earth, although this time it will not end quickly. It is the wrath of God poured out for seven horrendous years upon this world as described throughout most of the Book of Revelation and many of the prophetic books of the Bible. If one adds up how many die in the Great Tribulation judgments found in the Book of Revelation, well over half—probably over two-thirds of the world's population will perish! One-third die in just one judgment alone (Revelation 9:15, 18). Revelation 6:15-17 tells us: *[15] And the kings of the earth, and the great men, and the rich men, and the chief captains, and the mighty men, and every bondman, and every free man, hid themselves in the dens and in the rocks of the mountains; [16] And they said to the mountains and rocks, Fall on us, and hide us from the face of him that sitteth on the throne, and from the wrath of the Lamb: [17] For the great day of his wrath is come; and who shall be able to stand?* This statement is made at the very beginning of the seven years of God's wrath. Nothing like this has ever happened before.

Now let's analyze the key Scripture concerning the timing of the Rapture and the revealing of the Anti-Christ.

2 Thessalonians 2:1-12 (NIV): *¹ Concerning the coming of our Lord Jesus Christ and our being gathered to him, we ask you, brothers and sisters, ² not to become easily unsettled or alarmed by the teaching allegedly from us—whether by a prophecy or by word of mouth or by letter—asserting that the day of the Lord has already come. ³ Don't let anyone deceive you in any way, for that day will not come until the rebellion occurs and the man of lawlessness* [the Anti-Christ] *is revealed, the man doomed to destruction. ⁴ He will oppose and will exalt himself over everything that is called God or is worshiped, so that he sets himself up in God's temple, proclaiming himself to be God.*

*⁵ Don't you remember that when I was with you I used to tell you these things? ⁶ And now you know **what is holding him back,** so that he may be revealed at the proper time. ⁷ For the secret power of lawlessness is already at work; but the one who now **holds it back** [restrains— RSV] will continue to do so till he is **taken out of the way.** ⁸ And then the lawless one will be revealed, whom the Lord Jesus will overthrow with the breath of his mouth and destroy by the splendor of his coming. ⁹ The coming of the lawless one will be in accordance with how Satan works. He will use all sorts of displays of power through signs and wonders that serve the lie, ¹⁰ and all the ways that wickedness deceives those who are perishing. They perish because they refused to love the truth and so be saved. ¹¹ For this reason God sends them a powerful delusion so that they will believe* *the lie [12] and so that all will be condemned who have not believed the truth but have delighted in wickedness.*

Let's dissect this more difficult passage of Scripture; it is most challenging because we have pre-Rapture concepts (*our gathering unto him*—verse 1), then tribulation details concerning the Anti-Christ (verses 4-12), and finally Second Coming/end of the Great Tribulation ideas *(the coming of our Lord Jesus*—verses 1 and 8) all combined under the general theme of the Anti-Christ. First, the King James Version, among others, says in verse 3 that, *there will be a great falling away first.* We are also told in verse 7 that the Anti-Christ's lawless spirit is already at work on earth even before his full revelation; that's what we war against now! In verses 3 and 9, this lawless son of perdition [the KJV and RSV description of him], the Anti-Christ, is revealed with his partner, a beast called the false prophet, as spoken of in Revelation 13 and Revelation 19:20. This is the full manifestation of Satan's copycat trinity on earth, since he (Satan) has also been cast down to earth (Revelation 12:7-10) to join with the Anti-Christ and his false prophet. He hates God's law, people, and temple yet to be rebuilt. As bad as it is with his spirit of lawless anarchy running rampant now on earth, I sure don't want to be here when that happens! However, it is clear from verses 6-8 that the Anti-Christ is held back until God's perfect timing. There is a power that holds him back and continues to do so until this restraining power is *taken out of the way.*

What is this withholding or restraining power? Scholars disagree. Some say it is the power of the Holy Spirit. I disagree because Scripture tells us that only through the power of the Holy Spirit are people convicted of sin and come to repentance. John 16:7b-13a: *⁷ᵇ...the comforter...I will send him unto you. ⁸ And when he is come, he will reprove the world of sin, and of righteousness, and of judgment: ⁹ Of sin, because they believe not on me; ¹⁰ Of righteousness, because I go to my Father, and ye see me no more; ¹¹ Of judgment, because the prince of this world is judged. ¹² I have yet many things to say unto you, but ye cannot bear them now. ¹³ᵃ Howbeit when he, the Spirit of truth, is come, he will guide you into all truth...*

If the Holy Spirit is gone from the earth during the tribulation, then how does God continue to reach out to the world's rebellious people during that seven-year period? Why would God the Holy Spirit leave anyway? If God couldn't watch or be here for the Great Tribulation, why would He leave His beloved Church—the Bride of Christ here to endure such suffering? I believe that God can't use the Church to witness, since they have been raptured into heaven. Therefore, during this seven-year period of tribulation, God has to use new unique instruments to witness to the world, and He tells us about them: they are the 144,000 Jewish witnesses (Revelation 7), later two special evangelists (Revelation 11), and then a special angel (Revelation 14:6). During the Great Tribulation some people are saved, which would require the convicting power of the Holy Spirit.

If this restraining power is not the Holy Spirit, then I believe it must be the only other withholding power possible—the true Church—the Bride of Christ on earth. The presence and prayers of the Church have the power to withhold and restrain the manifestation of the Anti-Christ until God allows him to be openly revealed. Until the Rapture occurs, the Church must overcome the lawless spirit already at work on earth; moreover, the faithful Church must be the salt and light (Matthew 5:13-14) that preserves the carcass of this spiritually decrepit world, to keep full corruption from occurring. That's one reason why we pray in the Lord's Prayer—*deliver us from evil,* and we pray for God's *kingdom to come*—His millennial 1,000 year reign on earth from Jerusalem His capital. As Abraham interceded for Sodom & Gomorrah, and as Jonah finally witnessed to evil Nineveh to restrain God's judgment, then surely the Church also has intercessory power to restrain God's full tribulation judgment until the time that we are removed from the scene.

Another Scriptural reference about the Anti-Christ mentioned in 2 Thessalonians 2:4 is that the Jewish temple is rebuilt (Rev. 11:1-2). As of the writing of this book, that has not happened yet, but one group of Israeli Jews has fully prepared all building materials, furniture, and priestly implements for that soon-coming event; I have visited Israel several times and have been blessed to see their preparations with my own eyes. Many prophetic teachers believe that Israel makes a peace treaty with the Anti-Christ at the start of the tribulation; this event in Scripture is called an *"agreement*

with hell" (Daniel 9:27, 11:21-24, and Isaiah 28:15 & 18). 2
Thessalonians 2:4 is when the Anti-Christ breaks this agreement half-way or three-and-a-half years into the seven years
of tribulation (Revelation 11:2, Revelation 12:6, Revelation
13:5, Daniel 7:25, Revelation 12:14). He causes the Jewish
sacrifices at the temple to cease when he commits *"an abomination of desolation"*—the worship of himself (Daniel 8:11
and 9:27) and very likely will sacrifice a pig as his historic
predecessor Antiochus Epiphanes did.

Revelation 13 confirms 2 Thessalonians 2:9 about
Satan's copycat power to do miracles and signs and wonders through the Anti-Christ, along with the help of his false
prophet. This is Satan's copycat trinity on earth—a copy of
God's kingdom.

Christ, in 2 Thessalonians 2:8 (NIV), will *"overthrow
[Satan's kingdom] with the breath of his mouth and destroy by the splendor of his [2nd] coming"* (Daniel 7:9-14,
Revelation 19:11-20). Revelation 19:20: *"and the beast...
and the false prophet... were cast alive into the lake of fire..."*

Conclusive New Testament Proofs That the Rapture Precedes the Tribulation

Among prophecy-believing Christians today, there is
a certain amount of pre-, mid-, and post-tribulation debate
concerning the Rapture. The key question concerning this

debate, I believe, is—will God judge the righteous Church along with the unrighteous world? In the **"Why"** section of our study, we have already looked at Old Testament Scriptures and foreshadowing examples as proof that God removed His faithful before various judgments. Now we will study New Testament Scriptures showing why I believe in a pre-tribulation Rapture.

Romans 5:9: *Much more then, being now justified by his blood, we shall be **saved from wrath** through him.*

1 Thessalonians 1:10: *And to wait for his Son from heaven, whom he raised from the dead, even Jesus, which **delivered us from the wrath** to come.*

1 Thessalonians 5:9: *For **God hath not appointed us to wrath,** but to obtain salvation by our Lord Jesus Christ,*

In all three of these Scriptures, this wrath to come from which we are delivered can only be either eternal damnation or the Great Tribulation that is coming to the earth. Let's continue on for more Scriptural evidence of the latter.

For example, in 1 Thessalonians 5:9 above, we know that Paul is talking about the Rapture because of his *thief in the night* comment, his *sudden destruction* cometh comment, and comments like the notable command to *watch and be sober* which we read in 1 Thessalonians 5:1-8 earlier in *The "Thief in the Night" Scenario* section of this book.

Luke 21:34-36: *[34] And take heed to yourselves, lest at*

any time your hearts be overcharged with surfeiting [hearts dulled by careless ease, carousing, partying, overindulgence, gluttony, gratification to excess], *and drunkenness, and cares of this life, and so that day* [Rapture, tribulation] *come upon you unawares.* ³⁵ *For as a **snare** shall it come on all them that dwell on the face of the whole earth.* ³⁶ ***Watch** ye therefore, and pray always, that ye may **be accounted worthy to escape** all these things that shall come to pass, and to stand before the Son of man.* If it were a mid- or post-tribulation Rapture, then the phrase *as a **snare*** would not apply; it would be a relief because the tribulation was coming to an end. Instead, we are told that a sudden, painful, deadly trap to the whole world shall come, and we can **escape** it.

Some critics of pre-tribulation belief say: "Well, you just want to escape all the bad times coming to this earth." Well, isn't that what God just told us that He wants for us in all of these verses? Besides, we aren't escaping the end times *beginning of sorrows* [*horrors* (Living)], a period during which Jesus listed all of the severe problems that would be coming on this earth in the end times just before the Rapture and the Great Tribulation (Matthew 24:5-13).

Again, notice all the character traits being mentioned of those who are to escape—such as those who take heed, watch, pray, and are worthy. The disciple Luke is definitely indicating that escape is conditional upon these qualities or characteristics that we will discuss in the **"Who"** will be raptured section.

Another deliverance promise from God was given to the faithful Church of believers at Philadelphia, which had no negative things said about it. Christ said in Revelation 3:10-11 (NKJ): *[10] Because you have kept My command to persevere, I also will **keep you from the hour of trial** [many English translations use words such as: testing, temptation, time of trouble, and Living uses: **time of Great Tribulation**], which shall come upon the whole world, to test those who dwell on the earth. [11] Behold, I come quickly!* Hold fast *what you have, that no one may take your crown.*

Revelation Chapters 2 and 3 are admonitions to seven actual historical churches in Turkey; many scholars also believe that they can be referred to as periods or eras of Church history. The word "church" or "churches" is mentioned seventeen times in Chapters 2 and 3 and never again until Revelation 22:16, the fifth-to-the-last verse in the Bible. Why is this? Is it not because the rest of Revelation is about the Great Tribulation during which the Church is not present to be judged or punished with the unfaithful world? That's why our test time is now. We are freely given the choice to separate from evil things and the distractions of this world during this *beginning of sorrows* time when the spirit of lawlessness of the Anti-Christ plagues the earth.

Immediately after Chapters 2 and 3 of Revelation, the disciple John, in Revelation 4:1, wrote: *After this I looked, and, behold, a door was opened in heaven: and the first **voice** which I heard was as it were of a **trumpet** talking with* *me; which said, **Come up hither**...* This is very similar to wording in our first reference verses concerning the Rapture found in 1 Thessalonians 4:16-17: *[16] For the Lord himself shall descend from heaven with a shout, with the **voice** of the archangel, and with the **trump**[et] of God... [17] We which are alive and remain shall be **caught up** to meet the Lord in the air.* We then see, in Revelation 4:4, twenty-four elders around the throne. I believe these represent or are symbolic of the Old Testament Jewish faithful (represented by the twelve tribes of Israel) and the faithful Church (represented by the twelve disciples of Christ) who are united in heaven from this point on.

In Revelation 5:9, we see the Church, redeemed to God by Christ's blood *out of every kindred, and tongue, and people, and nation,* singing and worshipping around the throne. The Great Tribulation begins only after the horrific tribulation seals are allowed to be opened when the Lamb of God is revealed to also be the Lion of the Tribe of Judah. Then the Anti-Christ is revealed to the world in Revelation Chapter 6 in the four phases of his reign on earth or what is now infamously called "the four horsemen of the apocalypse." Most all the rest of the Book of Revelation is about these tribulation horrors being poured out upon the world.

Even in the midst of the Great Tribulation, however, we see God's mercy poured out in Revelation 7 when 144,000 Jews (12,000 from each of the twelve tribes of Israel) preach the Gospel and many are led to the Lord and become the tribulation saints mentioned in verses 9-14 of that same chapter. Later, in Revelation 11, even during His wrath on the earth, God continues to reach out to the world through His two special witnesses or evangelists. For one last merciful tribulation gleaning, God uses a special angel *having the everlasting gospel to preach unto them that dwell on the earth, and to every nation, and kindred, and tongue, and people* (Revelation 14:6). God has never used an angel to preach the gospel before, but He has to now because the Church is in heaven. These latter tribulation saints pay the dear price when they are beheaded by the Anti-Christ (Revelation 20:4) in order to join the Old and New Testament saints already in heaven. I feel that these tribulation saints references bring confusion to people concerning pre- or mid-tribulation beliefs. I wonder how many of these tribulation saints are ones who knew the truth, yet lived foolishly and carelessly and were not ready and missed the Rapture earlier. Now they become convicted of their need to be serious with God. Romans 1:18 (NKJ) says: *For the wrath of God is revealed from heaven against all ungodliness and unrighteousness of men, who suppress the truth in unrighteousness.*

Why are these three special groups of witnesses needed? If the Church is still on earth, why isn't it the Church that is doing this witnessing? Is it not because the Church is already in heaven from Revelation Chapter 4 on, joined as the Bride to our Savior, Jesus Christ?

Some argue that it will take the Great Tribulation to purify the Church to bring it to its correct place as the Bride of Christ. I don't believe so, and I don't think they really understand what the Great Tribulation is all about or how horrendous it will be. In a true love relationship, force is not a method to gain love; choice or freedom to choose God versus this world is always what God places in front of all of mankind. Choice is always given by God or else God would have just created a bunch of robots to repeat constantly to Him, "I love you, I love you, I love you," over and over again. That would be totally worthless worship to God or anyone else for that matter.

To every one of the seven churches in Revelation Chapters 2 and 3, Jesus our Lord commanded them to **overcome** their particular earthly and spiritual circumstances and problems. To the church of Thyatira, He said: *...I am he who searches deep within men's hearts, and minds; I will give to each of you whatever you deserve* (Revelation 2:23—Living).

To the church of Ephesus, which had left its first love of God, God said, *Remember therefore from whence thou are fallen, and repent, and do the first works...* (Revelation 2:5a). God gives the Church a choice of whether or not to repent.

Again, He told the church of Philadelphia that **He would keep them...from the time of Great Tribulation and temptation,** *which will come upon the world...* (Revelation 3:10—Living). Luke 21:36 says: *...that we may be **accounted***

worthy to escape *...* 1 Thessalonians 5:9 says: *God hath **not** appointed us to wrath* [tribulation]... We have a different appointment—a wedding appointment!

Why does Satan fight so hard to deceive us and try to keep us unfocused concerning the Rapture? Scripture says that he is the deceiver who comes to steal, kill, and destroy (John 10:10). If he can deceive us, destroy our blessed hope, and trap us in the snares of this world, then we will have chosen to slide into the judgment that God determined only for this world. The tribulation will kill roughly two-thirds of the world's population—one-third of mankind in just one punishment (the sixth trumpet—Revelation 9:15-18). Satan would love to "have at you" during that horrific seven years. Martyrdom or being beheaded for Christ is the only way to be redeemed during this period of time. Isn't getting serious with God now a much better scenario? Lastly, summarizing all of the previous work in this section of the book, I believe the Rapture is before the Great Tribulation (or pre-trib) for reasons and concepts that we have already established such as:

- We wouldn't need to be **discerning the signs of the times** if we were in the midst of or at the end of the Great Tribulation. We wouldn't be wondering if the storm was coming; instead, we would be in the midst of the hurricane. The Book of Revelation would tell us about the next judgment to come. There would be nothing to discern.

- It wouldn't be a **"thief in the night" scenario** in which, after the world proclaims *peace and safety,* then *sudden destruction cometh* or follows immediately if it was a mid- or post-tribulation situation. There would not have been *peace and safety* for we would have already seen massive worldwide destruction and the death of many hundreds of millions. Neither would it be something that we have to **watch** for if the Rapture occurred mid- or post-tribulation. We know the opening scene of the tribulation (Israel's treaty/agreement with hell—the Anti-Christ) and we know the midpoint of the tribulation (the Anti-Christ's abomination of desolation of Israel's temple worship) at which time Israel must immediately flee to the wilderness (most likely in and around Petra). [Revelation 12:13-14, 13:5; Daniel 8:11, 9:27, 11:41; Matthew 24:15-22]

- The pre-tribulation view is really the only viewpoint that believes in the imminent or sudden, unexpected coming of Christ which we are told over and over again to be watching and waiting and prepared for. Since we know the timing of tribulation events, and if we were here on earth for the Great Tribulation, all of our focus would be on the Anti-Christ and the judgments coming on the earth. Nowhere in Scripture are we told to watch for the Anti-Christ. We are only told to watch for Christ our Bridegroom.

- The **Father's long delay** (Matthew 24:48 and 25:19) of His Son's coming can't happen in a set seven-year tribulation scenario. You can't delay a seven-year time period once it has begun; delay can only occur before it starts.

- The list of fruits, qualities, or characteristics of those who are ready for the Rapture would no longer apply. We are going to examine that list in a much more concise and deeper way now in the culminating section of this book on **"Who"** will be raptured.

VI. WHO? — Who Will Be Raptured?

Surprisingly, the big controversy in the Church should not be **"when"** the Rapture shall occur, but **"who"** shall be taken. We can become **distracted by "when" questions** when we really should **be more concerned by the "who" questions.** Could this be a distraction from our enemy?

It may surprise you to discover that if you have been seriously taking into the depths of your heart each of the underlined characteristics given in well over one hundred verses already quoted in this book that God implores us to have in our lives, then much of the **"Who"** will be raptured has already been absorbed. It's now time to take all the pieces of the puzzle, assemble them together, and see the big picture.

It is EXTREMELY IMPORTANT to realize that these are not works of the law or a legalistic religious life. They are the resultant **fruits, qualities, or characteristics of the Spirit of God** who has worked a miracle of grace in someone's life. The next several pages are a compilation (but on a much larger scale) of what is given to us in Galatians 5:22-23 (also listed in 2 Peter 1:5-8) of *the fruit of the spirit...against such there is no law.* The Holy Spirit produces fruit in a believer like love, joy, peace, faith, righteousness, goodness, patience (longsuffering), a sober, pure, and separate life from the world (temperance), humbleness (meekness), etc. This is not by man's works, but is the fruit or outer manifestation of God's inner workings in men's and women's hearts and lives. It's a heart issue.

Jesus said in Matthew 7:16 (NKJ) that *"You will know them by their fruits. Do men gather grapes from thorn bushes or figs from thistles?* I want to be fruit that He gathers on that special day—the Rapture. Philippians 1:9-11 (NKJ) tells us: *⁹ And this I pray, that your love may abound still more and more in knowledge and all discernment, ¹⁰ that you may approve the things that are excellent, that you may be sincere and without offense **till the day of Christ,** ¹¹ being **filled with the fruits of righteousness,** which are by Jesus Christ, to the glory and praise of God.*

𝒥𝓇𝓊𝒾𝓉𝓈, 𝒬𝓊𝒶𝓁𝒾𝓉𝒾𝑒𝓈, 𝑜𝓇 𝒞𝒽𝒶𝓇𝒶𝒸𝓉𝑒𝓇𝒾𝓈𝓉𝒾𝒸𝓈 𝒪𝒻 𝒯𝒽𝑜𝓈𝑒 𝒲𝒽𝑜 𝒲𝒾𝓁𝓁 𝑩𝑒 𝑹𝒶𝓅𝓉𝓊𝓇𝑒𝒹

The following are the **fruits, qualities,** or **characteristics** (and their relevant Scriptures) that we have studied and underlined throughout this book related to the Rapture. These are the characteristics of those that God says He will "catch up" or Rapture to be with Him. Any Scriptures found in [brackets] are yet to be studied in this book.

➤ LOVE THE LORD WITH ALL ONE'S HEART, SOUL, MIND—Matthew 22:37-38, 1 Peter 1:8

- ➤ LOVE GOD FIRST RELATIONSHIP—John 14:3, Romans 11:22, Revelation 2:4, Matthew 22:37-38, 1 Corinthians 2:9

- ➤ FEAR, LOVE, AND SERVE THE LORD, OBSERVE HIS WORD—Deuteronomy 10:12-13

- ➤ BY FAITH/TRUSTING/BELIEVING—Hebrews 11:5-7, Hebrews 10:23, Romans 11:22, 1 Peter 1:8, 2 Corinthians 5:7, [Ephesians 2:8-10, 1 Thessalonians 2:13b]

- ➤ SOBER, FAITH, LOVE, HOPE—Hebrews 10:23-25, 1 Thessalonians 5:8, Revelation 3:10-11, Titus 2:12-13

- ➤ BE AT PEACE—1 Thessalonians 5:13, [2 Peter 3:14]

- ➤ HOLY— Ephesians 5:27, 2 Peter 3:14-17

- ➤ WALK HUMBLY, OBEY, AND DO WHAT IS RIGHT— Zephaniah 2:2-3

- ➤ BE PATIENT—James 5:7-8 (2 times), 1 Thessalonians 5:14

- ➤ FAITHFUL AND WISE—Matthew 24:45-46, [Matthew 7:24-25, Matthew 25:1-13, Ephesians 5:15-17]

- ➤ KNOW THE LORD—Hosea 2:19-20

- ➤ ABIDE IN CHRIST—1 Thessalonians 4:16-18, 1 John 3:1-3, Ephesians 2:13, [John 15:1-5, 8]

- ➤ BORN AGAIN/CONVERTED/SAVED/NEW PERSON—Romans 7:4, [John 3:3, Matthew 18:3, Ephesians 2:8-10]

- ➤ CONFESS OUR ACCEPTANCE—Romans 10:9

- ➤ MADE NIGH BY THE BLOOD OF CHRIST—Ephesians 2:13

- ➤ BUILT HIS LIFE (HOUSE) ON THE ROCK (JESUS)— [Matthew 7:24-27]

> PLEASED GOD—Hebrews 11:5

> WALKED WITH GOD—Genesis 5:24, 6:9

> OBEDIENT—Zephaniah 2:2-3

> SET AFFECTIONS ON THINGS ABOVE (HEAVEN)—Colossians 3:2

> LOVE LESS THE THINGS OF THIS WORLD/ FORSAKE ALL—Luke 14:25-27, 33

> WITHOUT SPOT, WRINKLE, OR BLEMISH, BLAMELESS—Ephesians 5:27, [2 Peter 3:14-15]

> PURE VIRGIN/PURIFIETH HIMSELF—2 Corinthians 11:2, 1 John 3:1-3, [Matthew 25:1-13]

> COME OUT AND BE SEPARATE FROM UNBELIEV-ERS—2 Corinthians 6:14-18

> LIVE SOBERLY, RIGHTEOUSLY AND GODLY/ DENY UNGODLINESS AND LUST—Titus 2:12-13, Revelation 19:7-9

> ABSTAIN FROM AND TURN AWAY FROM LAST DAYS' EVILS—2 Timothy 3:1-7, 1 Thessalonians 5:22

> PRAY WITHOUT CEASING—1 Thessalonians 5:17, Luke 21:36, Luke 18:1, [Colossians 4:2, Ephesians 6:18, Nehemiah 4:9, Mark 13:33]

> ARISE, AWAKE—Song of Solomon 2:10, 13, [Romans 13:11b-14, Ephesians 5:14]

> BE ACCOUNTED WORTHY TO ESCAPE—Luke 21:34-36

> BE NOT SPIRITUALLY ASLEEP—1 Thessalonians 5:6

> BE READY, PREPARED, KEEP YOUR GARMENTS PREPARED—Revelation 16:15, 19:7-9, Matthew 24:44, Hebrews 11:7, [Matthew 25:9-11]

➢ BEWARE LEST WE FALL FROM OUR STEADFAST-NESS—2 Peter 3:14-17, [Hebrews 3:14]

➢ WAIT AND HEAR/LISTEN TO GOD—John 3:29, Luke 10:38-42, [Revelation 3:20]

➢ HAS AN EAR TO HEAR WHAT THE SPIRIT SAYS— [Luke 8:8b, 18a, 14:35, each of the seven churches in Revelation Chapters 2 and 3]

➢ STUDY AND WASHED BY HIS WORD— Matthew 4:4, Ephesians 5:26, [John 15:3, 2 Timothy 2:15]

➢ TAKE HEED (hearts not overcharged with surfeiting, drunkenness and cares of this life)—Luke 21:34, Mark 13:33, Romans 11:21, [Hebrews 3:12]

➢ DISCERN THE SIGNS OF THE TIMES—Matthew 16:2-3

➢ A SERVANT DOING THE MASTER'S WILL—Matthew 24:45-46, Mark 13:32-37, [Matthew 7:21-24, Ephesians 5:17]

➢ DOING THE WORK OF THE LORD—[Nehemiah 4:16-18, Ephesians 2:10]

➢ PRODUCE FRUIT AND GOOD DEEDS—Romans 7:4, [Luke 8:15, 13:6-9, John 15:1-5, 8, Ephesians 2:10, Revelation 2:2-5]

➢ A LIGHT TO THE WORLD—Matthew 5:14-16, 25:1-13, Proverbs 13:9

➢ PREACH THE GOSPEL TO ALL THE WORLD—Matthew 24:14

➢ EXHORT AND PROVOKE ONE ANOTHER UNTO FAITH, LOVE, AND GOOD WORKS—Hebrews 10:23-25

> COMFORT ONE ANOTHER—1 Thessalonians 4:18, 5:11

> BE PATIENT, COMFORT, AND SUPPORT THE WEAK AND FEEBLEMINDED—1 Thessalonians 5:14

> FEAR HIM AND WORK RIGHTEOUSNESS—Revelation 19:7-9, Acts 10:34-35, Hebrews 11:7, Deuteronomy 10:12

> BE HUMBLE, NOT HIGHMINDED, BUT FEAR (fear of the Lord)—Zephaniah 2:2-3, Romans 11:20, Hebrews 11:7, [Philippians 2:3-4]

> BE FILLED WITH THE HOLY SPIRIT—[Ephesians 5:18]

> QUENCH NOT THE SPIRIT, DESPISE NOT PROPHESYINGS—1 Thessalonians 5:19-20

> COUNT THE COST/FINISH YOUR WALK/BEAR YOUR CROSS—[Luke 14:28-33]

> DENY YOURSELF/TAKE UP YOUR CROSS AND FOLLOW ME—[Matthew 16:24-26]

> STIR UP (hearts and minds)—Hebrews 10:24, 2 Timothy 1:6, 2 Peter 3:1, 5, 8 (be not ignorant)

> STEADFAST, UNMOVEABLE—1 Corinthians 15:58, 2 Peter 3:17, [Hebrews 3:6-19]

> HOLD FAST, PERSEVERE, BE DILIGENT, STAND FIRM—Hebrews 10:23, Revelation 3:2-3, 10-11, [2 Peter 3:14, 1 Corinthians 16:13, Revelation 2:2-5, Luke 18:1-8, Ephesians 6;13, Hebrews 3:6-19]

> PUT ON THE WHOLE ARMOR OF GOD/WRESTLE AGAINST SPIRITUAL WICKEDNESS—[Ephesians 6:11-12, Nehemiah 4:7-17]

- OVERCOME—To each of the seven churches of Revelation Chapters 2 and 3.

- BE SOBER, BE VIGILANT—[1 Peter 5:8]

- BE COURAGEOUS/BE NOT AFRAID/BE STRONG— [1 Corinthians 16:13, Ephesians 5:10-13, Nehemiah 4:14, Ephesians 6:10]

- ENDURE HARDSHIP AND SUFFERING—[2 Timothy 2:3-4, Revelation 2:2-5]

- WALK CIRCUMSPECTLY—[Ephesians 5:15, Exodus 23:13]

Saving the most important for last, the following two characteristics are related to each other, are by far the most quoted, and therefore we assume they are the most important. They definitely should be part of our lives, but further study and understanding must occur for us to truly comprehend the depth of their meaning:

- LOOKING FOR HIS COMING—[2 Peter 3:12a, 14, Hebrews 9:28, Titus 2:12-13, 2 Timothy 4:8]

- WATCH (watch and pray)—Matthew 24:42-51, 1 Thessalonians 5:6, Luke 21:36, Mark 13:32-37, Revelation 3:2-3, 16:15 (watch is used over a dozen times in the above Scriptures alone), Matthew 25:13, [Ephesians 6:18, 1 Corinthians 16:13, Proverbs 8:34, Colossians 4:2, Nehemiah 4:9, 7:3]

Since this composite list of characteristics is from well over one hundred Scripture verses, it looks overwhelming to even the seasoned Christian. Understand, however, that no single fruit tree can bring forth all types of fruits.

Every fruitful tree is different, and every fruitful believer will exemplify their fruits in unique ways and to differing degrees. As God works His work in you, His fruit will blossom forth. With God's grace and help, however, we may want to set our sights on some areas of personal improvement to become a better Bride-to-be. Remember, we are not under the law, but we are under and IN our husband-to-be—the Lord Jesus Christ. Fruit grows in those who abide IN Christ and who allow God to work in their lives.

Romans 7:4: *Wherefore, my brethren, ye also are become dead to the law by the body of Christ; that ye should be **married** to another, even to him who is raised from the dead, that **we should bring forth fruit unto God.***

Having now studied all of the fruits, qualities, or characteristics given in Scripture relating to the Rapture, [11b]... **what manner of persons ought ye to be [or become]**... [12a] **Looking for** and hasting unto the coming of the day of God... (2 Peter 3:11b-12a).

Jesus had much to say about fruit or being fruitful. In the Parable of the Sower in Luke 8:5-8, 11-15, and 18 (also in Matthew 13:3-9, and 18-23), God sowed seed or the Word of God throughout the world. There are four types of hearers or receivers of the Word. The devil stole the Word from the first group who had hard hearts. During times of temptation, tribulation, or persecution the seed also withered away from those in the second group who had no depth or root in themselves or in the Word of God. Then Luke 8:14-15 tells us of the two other categories of hearers of the Word. *[14] And that which fell among thorns are they, which, when they have heard, go forth, and are choked with cares and riches and pleasures of this life and **bring no fruit to perfection**. [15] But that on the good ground are they, which in an honest and good heart, having heard the word, keep it, and **bring forth fruit with patience**.* Fruit takes digging, planting, weeding, watering, sun (the Son), and patience. For myself, my culture, my nation—I feel that verse 14 is our greatest challenge!

At the end of the parable, Christ continued on to caution His followers with this challenge found in Luke 8:8b and 18a: *[8b] ...he cried, He that hath ears to hear, let him hear. [18a] Take heed therefore how ye hear:...* This is the same caution or challenge given to each of the seven churches of Revelation Chapters 2 and 3. Is the Church, then and now, hard of hearing?

In Matthew 21:18-22, Jesus cursed a fruitless fig tree. He did this as a lesson about having faith and about being fruitful. He even taught a parable about the barren fig tree in Luke 13:6-9 about being fruitful, in which He said *...I come seeking fruit*—fruit like that summarized on the previous half-dozen pages. Jesus demands these spiritual fruits of a born again/changed life.

John 15:1-5, 8 (NKJ): *¹ I am the true vine, and My Father is the vinedresser. ² Every branch in Me that does not bear fruit he takes away; and every branch that **bears fruit** He prunes, that it may **bear more fruit.** ³ You are already clean because of the word which I have spoken to you. ⁴ **Abide in Me,** and I in you. As the branch cannot bear fruit of itself, unless it abides in the vine, neither can you, unless you <u>abide in Me</u>. ⁵ I am the vine, you are the branches. He who abides in Me, and I in him, **<u>bears much fruit;</u>** for without Me you can do nothing... ⁸ By this My Father is glorified, that you **bear much fruit;** so you will be My disciples.*

Jesus is the Word (John 1:1). The previous list of fruits, qualities, or characteristics of those who will be raptured was compiled straight out of the Word—therefore, from Jesus himself. These qualities are what Jesus is looking for in His Bride-to-be. Doesn't He get to say who will be His Bride just as you or I do? These are, after all, the qualities, characteristics, or fruits of those who you also want to spend eternity with in your heavenly family.

God will not have the opposite in heaven. How can I say this? Revelation 21:27 (NKJ) says: *But there shall by no means enter it* [the New Jerusalem, heaven] *anything that defiles, or causes an abomination or a lie, but only those who are written in the Lamb's Book of Life.* The antithesis or the opposite of the fruits of the spirit (Galatians 5:22-23) are the works of the flesh found in Galatians 5:19-21 (NKJ): *¹⁹ Now the works of the flesh are evident which are: adultery, fornication, uncleanness, licentiousness,* [20] *idolatry, sorcery, hatred, contentions, jealousies, outbursts of wrath, selfish ambitions, dissensions, heresies,* [21] *envy, murders, drunkenness, revelries, and the like; of which I tell you beforehand, just as I also told you in time past, that those who practice such things will not inherit the kingdom of God.* By grace let us confess any of these before God, and ask Him to remove them from our lives that we may live with Him and the saints in eternity. Paul ended his tough message with: *those who are Christ's have crucified the flesh with its passions and desires.* [Galatians 5:24 (NKJ)].

The Conditional Nature of the Rapture

Come now, let us reason together. Will everyone who lives in a supposedly Christian nation be included in the Rapture? Geographers say that almost two billion out of seven billion people on earth in the year 2015 live in Christian regions or countries. Many so-called people of the Christian cultural world are labeled Christian simply by their physical birthplace. For example, they may have been born into Christian Europe or North or South America, which are generally classified as Christian regions because a majority, but definitely not all, of their people espouse that particular religion. Were Hitler or Stalin Christians simply because they were born in a Christian region or nation? Their beliefs and their later actions proved that they were not; they were the antithesis thereof. Is all of the United States Christian? Will all of the United States be raptured en masse?

Today Christianity has all but disappeared in Turkey where the seven churches of Revelation were located. If you have studied or visited Europe, then it isn't a surprise to you to know that Christianity in Europe is almost dead, and its fire has also dwindled rapidly here in my country of America. Too often we *have a form of godliness but deny the power thereof* (2 Timothy 3:5). God continues this verse by telling us, *from such turn away.* Will Jesus sadly have to turn away from such on that climatic day—the Rapture? I'm glad I am not to be the judge of men's souls, but God must be. He is the righteous judge in whom we can trust.

Many of these so-called "cultural Christians" have never really taken the first steps and been "converted" spiritually or "born again" of the Spirit of God as Christ said that they must be. John 3:3 (NKJ): *Jesus answered and said to him, "Most assuredly, I say to you, unless one is **born again**, he cannot see the kingdom of God."* Matthew 18:3 (NKJ): *"Assuredly, I say to you, unless you are **converted**, and become as little children, you will by no means enter the kingdom of heaven."*

Going deeper, can one just say a quick sinner's prayer and continue on living for and of this world yet have a guarantee of being raptured and not judged with this world in the Great Tribulation? God, the omniscient judge, knows all [12b] ...*the thoughts and intents of the heart. ¹³ And there is no creature hidden from His sight, but all things are naked and open to the eyes of Him to whom we must give account* (Hebrews 4:12b-13 [NKJ]). Continuing the study of **"Who"** is going to be raptured will, I believe, answer this and further questions. Remember that throughout our inquiry, the Rapture or the catching up of His Bride leads to their marriage feast in heaven [Revelation 19:7]. Those who marry should do so because of a strong love relationship, not just a casual one-night acquaintance.

We cannot remind ourselves often enough of Jesus' first and great commandment in Matthew 22:37-38: *³⁷ Jesus said unto him, Thou shalt love the Lord thy God with all thy heart, and with all thy soul, and with all thy mind. ³⁸ This is the first and great commandment.* If our Bible was only two verses long, these would have to be the two verses and we should take this to heart.

Investigations and findings by the well-respected Barna Group (www.barna.org) may help us see this issue more clearly. This research group has actually polled and researched American and "Christian" beliefs and levels of religious dedication. They have been conducting and analyzing primary research to understand cultural trends related to values, beliefs, and behavior, especially among Christians, since 1984.

In their May 21, 2007 research report, it states: *Eighty-three percent of Americans identified themselves as Christians, yet only half or 49 percent of these described themselves as absolutely committed to Christianity.* [*Americans Stay Spiritually Active But Biblical Views Wane,* May 21, 2007]

Some of their more recent research shows that only 39 percent of these so-called Christians had participated in three normal religious activities such as attending church, prayer, and Bible reading, in the past week. [*Self-Described Christians Dominate America But Wrestle With Four Aspects of Spiritual Depth,* September 13, 2011.]

Over the years, The Barna Group has categorized "Christians" into two main groups— born again and Evangelical Christians. These two categories are *based upon their personal commitment to Christ as well as their theological perspectives.*

Born again Christians are defined as people who said they have made a personal commitment to Jesus Christ that is still important in their life today, and who also indicated they believe that when they die they will go to Heaven because they had confessed their sins and had accepted Jesus Christ as their Savior. The percentage of Americans whose beliefs are categorized as born again has tapered off somewhat; currently, 40 percent of born again Christians compare with 45 percent in last year's study (2006).

Within the born again group are Evangelical Christians, who also embrace an additional set of beliefs in addition to their profession of faith in Christ and confession of personal sinfulness. Those additional beliefs include saying their faith is very important in their life today; believing they have a personal responsibility to share their religious beliefs about Christ with non-Christians; believing that Satan exists; believing that eternal salvation is possible only through grace, not works; believing that Jesus Christ lived a sinless life on earth; asserting that the Bible is accurate in all that it teaches; and describing God as the all-knowing, all-powerful, perfect deity who created the universe and still rules it today. Being classified as an evangelical is not dependent upon church attendance or the denominational affiliation of the church attended. The May 21, 2007 study found that seven percent of adults qualify as to being what The Barna Group calls *Evangelical Christians...*

Most Americans [and may I add, Christians] *do not have strong and clear beliefs largely because they do not possess a coherent Biblical worldview. That is, they lack a consistent and holistic understanding of their faith.* Evidently, many are not being the wise men that we will read about in Matthew 7:24 who heard or read God's Word, believed it, and did as it commanded. This is happening even when Bibles, churches, and Christian media are available everywhere we turn.

The following key beliefs are how The Barna Group identifies those who they say are in the Evangelical category. [Important Note: the percentages which follow each statement are the percentages of so-called born again believers (not all Americans) who agree with the belief statement.]

- *Believe that the Bible is accurate in all the principles it teaches.* [79%]

- *Believe that God is the all-powerful, all-knowing Creator of the universe who still rules it today.* [93%]

- *Believe that Jesus Christ lived a sinless life.* [62%]

But less than half of "born again Christians" believed the following doctrinal statements:

- *Believe in absolute moral truth.* [46%]

- *Believe that Satan is a real force.* [40%]

- *Strongly reject the notion of earned salvation through their deeds or good works.* [47%]

Ongoing research by The Barna Group on these matters consistently demonstrates the powerful impact a person's worldview has on their life. A worldview serves as a person's decision-making filter, enabling them to make sense of the complex and huge amounts of information, experiences, relationships and opportunities they face in life. A worldview has a dramatic influence on a person's choices in any given situation. Barna's research has discovered that there are unusually large differences in behavior related to matters such as media use, profanity, gambling, alcohol use, honesty, civility, and sexual choices. [*Changes in World View Among Christians Over the Past 13 Years,* March 6, 2009.]

Before we look further into all of the other Scriptures which indicate the **conditional nature** concerning Christ's coming for His Bride, let's review one aspect of our previous study in Matthew 24:40-41: *[40] Then shall two be in the field; the one shall be taken, and the other left. [41] Two women shall be grinding at the mill; the one shall be taken, and the other left.* We know that Christ was talking about believers because He continues in the next dozen verses in the Parable of the Two Servants to exhort His believers to watch, be ready, be wise and faithful servants, and be doing the Master's will. Yet only half of the believers or servants are taken, and the other half are left with the hypocrites, weeping and gnashing their teeth.

Some Scriptural statements may seem to be hard pills to swallow, but like medicine from on high, they are meant for our well-being. This may not be popular teaching today, when many people can't stand sound doctrine, but isn't that simply another sign of the end times? Maybe that's why half of the so-called Church won't be ready. 2 Timothy 4:3-4 (Living) says: *[3] For there is going to come a time when people won't listen to the truth, but will go around looking for teachers who will tell them just what they want to hear. [4] They won't listen to what the Bible says but will blithely follow their own misguided ideas.* Scripture is Christ's exhortation to us, and we need to take it seriously. He loves us so, and He wants us to be ready for His coming.

Will everyone who calls themselves a Christian be raptured? Many may profess Christ, but some do not possess Christ. How many ceremoniously wear a cross around their neck next to their heart, while missing the born again heart relationship and the walk that God really desires? Many don't put their faith or lives into God's hands and walk with God daily. Many seldom read or study His Bible, and as a result they have no foundation and therefore do not believe in key doctrinal beliefs of the Church. They seldom pray, nor do they attend church regularly or take part in communion with Him. Some who do may just be going through religious ceremonies or traditions without a heartfelt bride type of love or relationship that God wants. Most importantly, they probably don't have any or many of the afore-listed fruits, qualities, or characteristics of spirit-converted or born again Christians. Will these people be part of the Rapture?

An even tougher question is, "Will all who really claim to know Him, yet not live accordingly, be 'caught up' in the Rapture and avoid God's Great Tribulation?" Lot's wife didn't make it. Only the few of Noah's family who actively lived and worked by faith on the ark were saved from God's period of judgment on the earth. Later parables in this last part of our study, I feel, will help answer this question.

As hard as it is to accept, Jesus said in Matthew 7:21-23: *²¹ Not every one that saith unto me, Lord, Lord, shall enter into the kingdom of heaven; but <u>he that doeth the will</u> of my Father which is in heaven. ²² Many will say to me in that day,*

*Lord, Lord, have we not prophesied in thy name? and in thy name have cast out devils? and in thy name done many wonderful works? ²³ And then will I profess unto them, **I never knew you:** depart from me, ye that work iniquity.*

To really **know** someone requires us to spend time with them, to talk to and listen to them, and be close to them in a personal relationship. To be called the Bride of Christ means that we are basically in a period of engagement down here on earth at this time. When I was engaged (over 40 years ago), it changed my whole life. My fiancée and I wanted to be together whenever possible; when apart, we wrote love letters and paid for costly long distance phone calls to each other. The spiritual equivalent of this would be constant communication with God—prayer, Bible study, believing, and following His love letters to us—the Bible—again, the **Basic Instructions Before Leaving Earth**.

Most assuredly, lest anyone think I am talking about salvation by works, Ephesians 2:8-10 (NKJ) says: *⁸ For by grace you have been saved through faith, and that not of yourselves; it is the gift of God, ⁹ Not of works, lest anyone should boast. ¹⁰ For we are His workmanship, created in Christ Jesus for good works, which God prepared beforehand that we should walk in them.* Study again the list of fruits, qualities, or characteristics given by God through many Scriptures; they are not a result of works, but the result of a grace-filled life and being truly in love with Christ.

You might wonder or argue—"How about babes in Christ who do not yet show the fruit of such character traits that take time and the patient work of God to develop?" Many or most Christians believe in an "age of accountability" which is different for all people. Paul mentions in 1 Corinthians 3:1-3 and Hebrews 5:12-14 that some Christians are in the milk stage of their walk in the Word, others are in the mature meat stage, and yet, sadly, there are still many others who aren't progressing as they should from the early milk to the more mature meat stage of spiritual life. God knows all. He knows where we are and the reasons why. He is a righteous Judge of all the thoughts and intentions of our heart. He will judge rightly.

These are important ideas and questions that each individual must answer. We want our hearts to be right and to be included in the Rapture and the wedding supper of our Lord. We don't want to miss being part of God's imminent prophetic event. God has the right to test us to see who really loves Him. As our righteous Judge, He has the right to question our lives and our motives. Someone once asked, "If you were on trial for being a Christian, would there be enough evidence or witnesses to convict you?" In this case, He knows all of our actions, our words, our thoughts—everything. Nothing is hidden from Him. Christ will judge Christians for rewards or commendations before his [bema] judgment seat.

Consider Romans 14:10b-12: *[10b] ...for we shall all stand before the* [bema] *judgment seat of Christ. [11] For it is written, As I live, saith the Lord, every knee shall bow to me, and every tongue shall confess to God. [12] So then every one of us shall give account of himself to God.*

2 Corinthians 5:10-11a (Living): *[10] For we must all stand before Christ to be judged and have our lives laid bare—before him. Each of us will receive whatever he deserves for the good or bad things he has done in his earthly body. [11a] It is because of this solemn fear of the Lord, which is ever present in our minds, that we work so hard to win others.* [For further study, read 1 Corinthians 3:1-15.]

For Christians, this judgment is not for condemnation or for salvation, but is for reward or commendation for the works that we have done unto God. Remember, we are redeemed and our Judge is also our defense lawyer, our advocate (1 John 2:1), our mediator (1 Timothy 2:5), and now He is our rewarder (Hebrews 11:6, Matthew 16:27, Revelation 22:12). While saved, some will suffer the loss of not receiving any rewards. This is a sobering concept because this is eternal; yet this is very joyous for those walking and working in the Lord's will. Many believe that this event will occur in conjunction with the Marriage Supper; we will need our crowns of reward in order to cast them before the King of Kings at the beginning of our time in heaven (Revelation Chapters 4 and 5).

We discussed Matthew 7:21-23 earlier; let us finish this passage with verses 24-27: *²⁴ Therefore whosoever <u>heareth</u> these sayings of mine, and <u>doeth</u> them, I will liken him unto a **wise** man, which <u>built his house upon a rock</u>: ²⁵ And the rain descended, and the floods came, and the winds blew, and beat upon that house; and it fell not: for it was founded upon a rock. ²⁶ And every one that heareth these sayings of mine, and doeth them not, shall be likened unto a **foolish man,** which built his house upon the sand: ²⁷ And the rain descended, and the floods came, and the winds blew, and beat upon that house; and it fell: and great was the fall of it.*

Scripture does not say if the rain, storms, or floods might come; the storms will come, even to America in these end times. Our only choice is to be wise and build upon the Rock Christ Jesus, or to go our own foolish way and watch everything crumble around us. My choice, and I pray it is yours also, is to build on the ROCK—Jesus Christ!

The Parable of the Ten Virgins

Many of you have probably been wondering when we would cover one of the two most important or enlightening parables of all. In Matthew 25:1-13 we find the **Parable of the Ten Virgins,** where we have further statements from

Jesus about foolish and wise humans. *¹ Then shall the kingdom of heaven be likened unto ten <u>virgins</u>, which took their lamps, and went forth to meet the bridegroom. ² And five of them were <u>**wise**</u>, and five were **foolish**. ³ They that were foolish took their lamps, and took no OIL with them: ⁴ But the wise took oil in their vessels with their lamps. ⁵ While the* **Bridegroom tarried, they all slumbered and slept.**

Let me interrupt in the middle of this parable to make a few expository comments. Virgins are pure—they haven't given themselves to the world or others. In the Greek, **wise** [G5429 Strong's Concordance—phronimos] means: thoughtful, cautious, and/or discreet. **Foolish** [G3474 Strong's Concordance—moros] means: heedless, blockheaded, and/or dull. Oil, many times in Scripture, represents the Holy Spirit. The lamp could be symbolic of a form of godliness, but without the power source—oil, in it, we have a worthless empty pot. This is a perfect illustration of 2 Timothy 3:5: *Having a form of godliness* [lamp], *but denying the power* [oil] *thereof: from such turn away.* As we studied earlier, in some Jewish/Eastern traditions, the bride must keep a small clay lamp (about half the size of a fist) burning in the window night after night until her bridegroom comes to find her. The small clay lamp has to be refilled daily; it is a sign of her faithfulness and readiness. It is symbolic of our need to be refilled daily with the Holy Spirit of God and God's Word. Paul says in 2 Corinthians 4:16b: *...though our outward man perish, yet the inward man is renewed day by day.*

While the bridegroom tarried, it caused a sleepiness to come over the virgins at just the wrong time. It is similar to when Jesus told His disciples to stay awake and pray on the most important night of world history; yet, they all fell asleep in the Garden of Gethsemane the night before His crucifixion (Luke 22:46). It's frightening to think that this could happen again in our time, just before the second visitation of the Messiah.

Continuing the Parable of the Ten Virgins in Mathew 25: *⁶ And at midnight there was a cry made, Behold, the **bridegroom cometh;** go ye out to meet him. ⁷ Then all those virgins arose, and trimmed their lamps. ⁸ And the foolish said unto the wise, Give us of your oil; for our lamps are gone out. ⁹ But the **wise** answered, saying, Not so; lest there be not enough for us and you: but go ye rather to them that sell, and buy for yourselves. ¹⁰ And while they went to buy, the bridegroom came; and they that **were ready** went in with him to the marriage: and the door was shut. ¹¹ Afterward came also the other virgins, saying, Lord, Lord, open to us. ¹² But he answered and said, Verily I say unto you, I know you not. ¹³ **Watch** therefore, for ye know neither the day nor the hour wherein the Son of man cometh.*

We have yet another command to watch, as well as another example of half being raptured into heaven. Just as in Matthew 7:21-24, our Lord again said, *"I know you not,"* to someone He expected a greater and more faithful relationship from. Sometimes in Scripture the verb *"to know"* has the connotation of a relationship equivalent to when a man knows his wife—an intimate marriage love relationship. Did these five foolish virgins not know or love God deeply enough to be intimate with God and be prepared as necessary? Did they only have a form of religion, but lack the depth of relationship with the Holy Spirit in their lives?

The foolish virgins may have begun the walk, but did not end it correctly; they did not walk daily, replenishing their oil—their power source—the Holy Spirit. In Hebrews Chapter 3 there is an exhortation to us brethren. God tells us several times in verses 6, 12 and 14 to take heed, hold fast… and be steadfast **unto the end.** He also warns us not to harden our hearts, but to remove all unbelief (verses 8, 12, 15 and 19). The Rapture will come. He will come for a wise, faithful Bride.

Many in the early Protestant Church of the 16th Century obviously had a fire in their heart to be wise virgins filled with the oil of the Spirit and prepared for His Coming. The Lutheran pastor Philipp Nicolai first wrote the words and music to *Wake, Awake, for Night is Flying.* Later, the famous Johann S. Bach made it a more popular hymn when he made changes to the words to improve its singability. Later, it went through further changes when it was translated from German into English. Here is the beginning of this great hymn:

Wake, **awake,** for night is flying;
The watchmen on their heights are crying:
Awake, Jerusalem, at last arise!
Midnight hears the welcome voices
And at the thrilling cry rejoices;
Come forth ye virgins, night is past,
The Bridegroom comes, **awake;**
Your lamps with gladness take;
And for His marriage feast prepare,
For ye must go to meet Him there.

Romans 13:11b-14 (NIV): *[11b] ...The hour has already come for you to **wake up** from your slumber, because our salvation is nearer now than when we first believed. [12] The night is nearly over; **the day is almost here.** So let us put aside the deeds of darkness and put on the armor of light. [13] Let us behave decently, as in the daytime, not in carousing and drunkenness, not in sexual immorality and debauchery, not in dissension and jealousy. [14] Rather, clothe yourselves with the Lord Jesus Christ, and do not think about how to gratify the desires of the flesh.*

Ephesians 5:14: ***Awake** thou that sleepest* [all you virgins who are asleep], *and **arise** from the dead* [literally or figuratively in the Greek], *and Christ shall give thee light* [put oil in your lamp].

While writing this book, one uncommon word "jumped" out at me. It has become a vital and key ideal for my life. It is found in the next verse—Ephesians 5:15: *See then that ye walk **circumspectly**, not as **fools**, but as **wise*** [servants, builders, and/or virgins]. Exodus 23:13 is the only other Biblical verse to use this word: *And in all things that I have said unto you be **circumspect**...* Since this word is not commonly used, let's look further into its meaning. Webster's Dictionary gives synonyms such as: wise, cautious, prudent, well behaved, careful, vigilant, and guarded. Strong's Concordance [H8104—samar (Hebrew), and G199—akribos (Greek)] expands the meaning further with: hedge around, protect, guard, beware, attend, take heed, keep, look narrowly, inspect, observe, persevere, wait diligently, perfectly, **watch,** and **watchman.**

It seems as if there are two parts in the word and maybe two lessons to be learned from this word "circumspectly." One is the "spect" part, which is the vigilant watching and guarding idea; the other is the "circum" part, which is the concept of a circumference or circle around us. We need to be focused on God, the center of our life, and we need Him to fence or hedge us around and guard us, while we cautiously stay in the center of His will. I also think of the concept that God wants our hearts to be circumcised unto Him. Deuteronomy 30:6 (NIV): *The Lord your God will circumcise your hearts and the hearts of your descendants, so that you may love him with all your heart and with all your soul, and live.*

So far, Ephesians 5 has told us to be awake and walk circumspectly. Why? Let's continue and find out in Ephesians 5:16-18, 25-27: *[16] Redeeming the time, because the days are evil. [17] Wherefore <u>be ye not unwise</u>* [servants, builders, and/or virgins], *but <u>understanding what the will of the Lord is</u>. [18] And be not drunk with wine, wherein is excess; but <u>be filled with the Spirit</u>* [oil in the lamp]; *[25] Husbands, love your wives, even as Christ also loved the church, and gave himself for it; [26] That he might sanctify and cleanse it with the washing of water by the word, [27] That he might present it to himself a glorious church, <u>not having spot, or wrinkle</u>, or any such thing; but that it should <u>be holy</u> and <u>without blemish</u>.* These qualities must be our aspiration.

The "Watch"

Remember the four watches of Mark 13:32-37: *[32] But of that day and that hour knoweth no man... [33] <u>Take ye heed</u>, <u>watch</u> and <u>pray</u>: for ye know not when the time is. [34] ...commanded the porter to <u>watch</u>. [35] <u>Watch</u> ye therefore: for ye know not when the master of the house cometh... [37] And what I say unto you I say unto all, <u>Watch.</u>*

"Watch" is the most important characteristic or command that Christ used in His exhortations concerning our readiness for His coming. Maybe the **"looking for"** and the much-used word **"watch"** (used in over a dozen Scriptures) is bothering you as much as it did me. Why?

When we think about it in the natural, how can we watch for a Rapture event that is over in an instant (in the twinkling of an eye), or is like a thief in the night? We can't see the event. Other than the signs leading up to it, what can we watch for?

The answer that I picture is a vigilant bride-to-be intently looking out her candle-lit window in anxious anticipation and yearning for her soon-coming bridegroom. Yes, she would be **watching for outward signs.** But the real key to this word, I believe, is that she would also need to **inwardly watch out** for her own total readiness. Is she bathed, is her wedding dress clean and ready? Is she packed up and ready to go? Has she said good-bye to her old family and world? Is the lamp lit every night marking her position and demonstrating her faithfulness to her lover?

Revelation 16:15a reveals this inward watching and preparation by the Bride: *Behold, I come as a thief. Blessed is he that **watcheth**, and keepeth his garments...*

A similar <u>watch</u> phrase which is used in relationship to the Rapture is **looking for.** We see, for example, 2 Peter 3:12 and 14 has **looking for** in it. See how it and Titus 2:12-13 are tied to inner fruits, qualities, or characteristics such as purity, peace, and righteousness.

2 Peter 3:12a and 14: *[12] **Looking for** and hasting unto the coming of the day of God... [14] Wherefore, beloved, seeing*

*that ye **look for** such things, <u>be diligent</u> that ye may be found of him <u>in peace,</u> <u>without spot,</u> and <u>blameless.</u>*

Titus 2:12-13: *[12] Teaching us that, <u>denying ungodliness</u> <u>and worldly lusts,</u> we should <u>live soberly, righteously, and</u> <u>godly,</u> in this present world; [13] **Looking for** that BLESSED HOPE, and the glorious appearing of the great God and our Saviour Jesus Christ;*

Notice—we are to be looking for Christ the King of Kings. Never once does Scripture tell us to look for the Anti-Christ. Consider also Hebrews 9:28: *...unto <u>them that</u> **look** <u>**for** him</u> shall he appear the second time...*

In the concordance, we glean further insight into the word **"watch."** In the Greek, watch [G1453 Strong's Concordance—egeiro, G1127—gregoreo and G69—agrypneo] means: to keep awake, be vigilant, collect one's faculties (eyes, ears, thinking), rouse from sleep or ruin, raise up, and awaken. But it also has an interesting military or police connotation. The military watch in the Greek [G5438 Strong's Concordance—phylake and G5442—phylasso] means: the act of guarding, a specific time to watch, isolation from normal society, to preserve, obey, avoid, keep, beware, observe, save. What are we guarding? We are to guard our hearts and our spiritual virginity for Christ, and hopefully we guard our family, loved ones, and friends around us for the same purpose. We are to take on a soldier's mentality. The following ten martial points may enlighten us.

A Soldier's Mentality and The Watch

These military-related mentalities and analogies are given with corresponding Scriptures and are similar in nature to the characteristics or mentality that we need to have concerning being ready or watching for the Rapture:

1. Soldiers live and actually must be prepared to die for a higher cause than themselves; they are under the authority of someone higher than themselves. Philippians 1:21: *For me to live is Christ, and to die is gain.* We must care enough about others to want to help protect them. 2 Timothy 2:3-4 (NIV): ³ *Join with me in <u>suffering</u> like a **good soldier** of Christ Jesus. ⁴ No one serving as a soldier gets entangled in civilian affairs, but rather tries to please his commanding officer.*

2. Soldiers are disciplined and are required to do daily exercise or workouts to stay physically strong. Christians need regular spiritual workouts in Bible study and prayer. 1 Corinthians 16:13 (RSV): *Be **Watchful,** <u>stand firm</u> in your faith, <u>be courageous,</u> <u>be strong</u>.* 2 Timothy 2:15: *<u>Study</u> to show thyself approved unto God, a workman that needeth not to be ashamed, rightly dividing the word of truth.*

3. Soldiers become part of a new team and take on a new family; the old family and friends, while loved, must often be painfully left behind but are definitely not forgotten.

The new combat team comes first with a "leave no one behind to the enemy" mentality. For Christians, *old things* [of life] *are passed away; behold, all things are become new.* (2 Corinthians 5:17). In many ways our new church friends become closer than family. Philippians 2:3-4 says: *³ ...but in lowliness of mind let each esteem others better than themselves. ⁴ Look not every man on his own things, but every man also on the things of others.* 2 Corinthians 6:14a says: *Be ye not unequally yoked together with unbelievers: for what fellowship hath righteousness with unrighteousness?*

4. A soldier's mentality becomes painfully aware that warfare (for Christians—spiritual warfare) is a constant and real threat because the enemy is always ready to strike; normal citizens usually don't have a feeling for this. There are enemies around who are not always easily detected. 1 Peter 5:8: *Be sober, be vigilant; because your adversary the devil, as a roaring lion, walketh about, seeking whom he may devour.*

5. Commanders sometimes order soldiers to get into isolated watchtowers, onto high ground, or on top of walls to stand **watch** or to stand guard. They/We stand above normal civilians' daily commerce and lifestyle. We live in the same nation, but our lifestyle is different from the rest. We have a different and higher calling. Soldiers belong to the king; we belong to our King of Kings. Proverbs 8:34: *Blessed is the man that heareth me, **watching** daily at my gates, waiting at*

the posts of my doors. Colossians 3:2 says: *Set your affection on things above, not on things on the earth.*

6. To stand **watch**—soldiers peer into the distance, sometimes using binoculars (even night vision) to enlarge their vision; their purpose is to scrutinize distant people (or enemies) and coming events up close long before others can imagine them. Proverbs 29:18: *Where there is no vision, the people perish...* Bible study (including prophecy) is a necessity.

7. Soldiers stay awake in different night **watches** while civilians get to sleep, play, and live normal lives. This implies that there is something worth protecting—our heavenly kingdom. There are four night watches—6-9 p.m. 9-midnight, 12-3 a.m., and 3-6 a.m. 1 Thessalonians 5:6: *Therefore let us not sleep as do others; but let us watch and be sober.* Colossians 4:2: *Continue in prayer, and watch in the same with thanksgiving.* Soldiers can face major penalties for falling asleep on duty—even death. We are called disciples; that word is associated with learning and understanding, which takes discipline.

8. Soldiers are expected to have self-control over normal desires. 1 Corinthians 6:19b: *...you are not your own.* We are in God's army now; we have a new master and lifestyle.

9. Soldiers must be willing to warn or awaken others who are in danger, even though they will be angry and in disbelief at you for disturbing their deadly slumber. Proverbs 6:10-11a: [10] *Yet a little sleep, a little slumber, a little folding*

of the hands to sleep: *[11a]So shall thy poverty* [or destruction] *come...* (Satan steals and kills). It is the death penalty for prophets not to warn the people (Ezekiel 3 and 33).

10. Soldiers keep their armor on and stay close to their weaponry at all times. Ephesians 6:10-13, 18: *[10] Finally, my brethren, be strong in the Lord, and in the power of his might. [11] Put on the whole armour of God, that ye may be able to stand against the wiles of the devil. [12] For we wrestle not against flesh and blood, but against principalities, against powers, against the rulers of the darkness of this world, against spiritual wickedness in high places. [13] Wherefore take unto you the whole armour of God, that ye may be able to withstand in the evil day, and having done all, to stand... [18] Praying always with all prayer and supplication in the Spirit, and watching thereunto with all perseverance and supplication for all saints.*

Around one percent of our nation of over 300 million plus people are active now in the military and would experience some or most of these mental and lifestyle shifts due to the nature of their occupation. But as you can see from the Scripture references following each concept, many of these ways of thinking or acting are how God wants us to be *as good soldiers of Christ Jesus* (2 Timothy 2:3).

An Old Testament example of this soldier mentality can be seen in Nehemiah 4:7-9, 13-18 (NIV) when Nehemiah was allowed to return to Israel to rebuild the walls around Jerusalem:

⁷ But when Sanballat, Tobiah, the Arabs, the Ammonites and the people of Ashdod heard that the repairs to Jerusalem's walls had gone ahead and that the gaps were being closed, they were very angry. ⁸ They all plotted together to come and fight against Jerusalem and stir up trouble against it. ⁹ But we <u>prayed</u> to our God and posted a guard **["watch"** in KJV] *day and night to meet this threat.¹³ Therefore I stationed some of the people behind the lowest points of the wall at the exposed places, posting them by families, with their swords, spears and bows. ¹⁴ After I looked things over, I stood up and said to the nobles, the officials and the rest of the people, "<u>Don't be afraid</u> of them. <u>Remember the Lord, who is great and awesome, and fight for your</u> families, your sons and your daughters, your wives and your homes."*
¹⁵ When our enemies heard that we were aware of their plot and that God had frustrated it, we all returned to the wall, each to our own work. ¹⁶ From that day on, half of my men <u>did the work</u>, while the other half were equipped with spears, shields, bows and armor. The officers posted themselves behind all the people of Judah ¹⁷ who were building the wall. Those who carried materials <u>did their work</u> with one hand and held a weapon in the other, ¹⁸ and each of the builders <u>wore his sword</u> at his side as he worked. But the man who sounded the trumpet stayed with me. Nehemiah 7:3b: *...appoint* **watches** *of the inhabitants of Jerusalem, every one in his* **watch,** *and every one to be over against his house.*

The Parable of the Great Wedding Supper (or the Parable of the Excuses)

The most fearsome of texts, especially for those of our American or Western lifestyle, is found in Luke 14:16-35 (and Matthew 22:1-14)—The **Parable of the Great Wedding Supper (or the Parable of the Excuses)**. Read both passages carefully. I will give you Luke's account of Jesus' parable.

Luke 14:16-35: *[16] Then said he unto him, A certain man made a great supper, and bade many: [17] And sent his servant at supper time to say to them that were bidden, Come; for all things are now ready. [18] And they all with one consent began to make* **excuse.** *The first said unto him, I have bought a piece of ground, and I must needs go and see it: I pray thee have me* **excused.** *[19] And another said, I have bought five yoke of oxen, and I go to prove them: I pray thee have me* **excused.** *[20] And another said, I have married a wife, and therefore I* **cannot come.**

In Matthew Chapter 22's account of this same event, God's invited people *made light of it.* In this context the word "light" is ameleo in the Greek [G272 Strong's Concordance] meaning: that they were careless of, were negligent of, or did not regard as important enough—to give correct priority to the Master's invitation. They went their ways, not necessarily into sin, but to their jobs and regular lifestyle—one to the farm (occupation), another to his merchandise, and another to his family. These are important, but not nearly as important as God or our spiritual and eternal lives. In Luke's account they ALL made **excuses** about possessions and riches, jobs and careers, and family being more important than the Lord.

I have experienced all of these types of excuses in my own life. Haven't you? During my long 14-month engagement to Norma, my bride-to-be, I had to ask forgiveness from the Lord for secret hopes that Christ wouldn't return and Rapture the Church before our wedding. I so wanted to be married down here on this earth, that I was putting it before my marriage to Him in heaven. Understandably, yet wrongly, I was putting worldly priorities before God. He wanted to refocus my priorities toward Him.

Later, my 80-100 hour per week teaching job and career kept interfering with my full service to God. He understood, yet lovingly kept encouraging me and helping me learn how to choose to put Him first. As we have prospered, like so many others in the United States, our home has become overwhelmingly blessed with merchandise and provisions; it has become near impossible not to be covetous—putting things and their spider-web like attractions and entanglements before God Almighty himself. The apostle Paul calls covetousness idolatry in Colossians 3:5. No wonder Christ said that it is nearly impossible for the rich to enter the kingdom of heaven. We must put God first in all aspects of our life.

As we continue, notice there is a delay [Matthew 22:9-10 and Luke 14:21-23] in the wedding supper while the Father gathers others not originally called on to come to the feast. Finishing the Parable of the Great Wedding Supper: *²¹ So that servant came, and shewed his lord these things. Then the master of the house being angry said to his servant, Go out quickly into the streets and lanes of the city, and bring in hither the poor, and the maimed, and the halt, and the blind. ²² And the servant said, Lord, it is done as thou hast commanded, and yet there is room. ²³ And the lord said unto the servant, Go out into the highways and hedges, and compel them to come in, that my house may be filled. ²⁴ For I say unto you, That none of those men which were bidden shall taste of my supper.*

As you have just read, this parable in Luke 14 ends shockingly, but Matthew 22's version is even more challenging. Matthew 22:11-14 says: *¹¹ And when the king came in to see the guests, he saw there a man which had not on a wedding garment: ¹² And he saith unto him, Friend, how camest thou in hither not having a wedding garment? And he was speechless. ¹³ Then said the king to the servants, Bind him hand and foot, and take him away, and cast him into outer darkness; there shall be weeping and gnashing of teeth. ¹⁴ For many are called, but few are chosen.*

I once thought the phrase *cast him into outer darkness; there shall be weeping and gnashing of teeth,* had only to do with hell which seemed extremely harsh in this case. I find this same phrase in the Parable of the Two Servants

(Matthew 24:45-51) discussed earlier, as well as in the Parable of the Talents (Matthew 25:14-30). I now conjecture that it may be referring not to hell but to missing the Rapture and therefore being doomed to going through the Great Tribulation which will be horrid. There surely will be weeping and gnashing (grinding) of teeth by those who are called of God, but who choose to make worldly excuses. Like Lot's wife, they love this world too much and have to experience judgment meant for the lost of this world only. The internal anguish would be excruciating.

After Christ finished the parable in Luke 14, it seems as if His Words become even more stern and challenging as He expounded on the parable further in verses 25-35: *²⁵ And there went great multitudes with him: and he turned, and said unto them, ²⁶ If any man come to me, and hate not [love less] his father, and mother, and wife, and children, and brethren, and sisters, yea, and his own life also, he cannot be my disciple. ²⁷ And whosoever doth not <u>bear his cross</u>, and come after me, cannot be my <u>disciple</u>.*

²⁸ For which of you, intending to build a tower, sitteth not down first, and <u>counteth the cost</u>, whether he have sufficient to finish it? ²⁹ Lest haply, after he hath laid the foundation, and is not able to <u>finish it</u>, all that behold it begin to mock him, ³⁰ Saying, This man began to build, and was not able to finish. ³¹ Or what king, going to make war against another king, sitteth not down first, and consulteth whether he be able with ten thousand to meet him that cometh against him *with twenty thousand?* ³² *Or else, while the other is yet a great way off, he sendeth an ambassage, and desireth conditions of peace.*

³³ *So likewise, whosoever he be of you that <u>forsaketh not all</u> that he hath, he cannot be my disciple.* ³⁴ *Salt is good: but if the salt have lost his savour, wherewith shall it be seasoned?* ³⁵ *It is neither fit for the land, nor yet for the dunghill; but men cast it out. He that hath **ears to hear, let him hear.***

We are to be faithful servants and disciples who are in love foremost with Him. He doesn't want our hearts to love things or even people over or above Him; this would be idolatry. We are to use our talents for God and make them multiply. This is not just God's wish for our lives, but His expectation for our lives. We are not our own anymore. We are bought by a tremendous price. Yes, salvation is free, but it may cost you everything. Matthew 16:24-27: ²⁴ *Then said Jesus unto his **disciples,** If any man will come after me, let him <u>deny himself,</u> and **take up his cross,** and <u>follow me.</u>* ²⁵ *For whosoever will save his life shall lose it: and whosoever will lose his life for my sake shall find it.* ²⁶ *For what is a man profited, if he shall gain the whole world, and lose his own soul? Or what shall a man give in exchange for his soul?* ²⁷ *For the Son of man shall come in the glory of his Father with his angels; and then he shall reward every man according to his works.*

I personally believe we are now in this period of "falling away" (2 Thessalonians 2:3), making excuses, and making light of the important things of God. Most of "Christian" Europe and the Americas have turned their backs on God. God's "latter rain" (James 5:7) ingathering is being poured out on the uttermost parts of the world like Africa and Asia. The Father may be angry at many of us (Luke 14:21) for making light of His call and with our worldly excuses!

What excuses do we make? Let me encourage you to do as God did with me. List excuses that you make for not putting God first:

1.

2.

3.

These excuses are not necessarily bad or evil; on the contrary—many are good things like family, jobs, and possessions. However, if we put them before God, they can become idols in our lives. We must repent and love these less. Turn your life back to your **first love—God.** Revelation 2:2-5 (NIV) says to the believers of the great church of Ephesus: ² *I know your deeds, your hard work and your perseverance.*

I know that you cannot tolerate wicked people, that you have tested those who claim to be apostles but are not, and have found them false. ³ *You have <u>persevered</u> and have <u>endured hardships</u> for my name, and have <u>not grown weary.</u>* ⁴ *Yet I hold this against you: You have* **forsaken the love you had at first.** ⁵ *Consider how far you have fallen! Repent and do the things you did at first. If you do not repent, I will come to you and remove your lampstand from its place.*

This book is all about a **love story**, even as the Bible itself is the all-time greatest selling love story in human history. Realize that the cares and pleasures of this life can choke out God, His Word (Luke 8:14), and His love. We have to come to a point in our lives where we love less or even hate (Luke 14:26) and/or forsake these barriers to God.

God ends the Parable of the Great Wedding Supper in Luke 14:35 with: **<u>*He that hath ears to hear, let him hear.*</u>** *"* Evidently, Jesus knows that some of His beloved followers can't believe their ears or won't listen to these words. They won't really hear or let the words sink fifteen inches from their ears and mind to their heart. You can't have changes in your life until after truly hearing the Word of God and letting it sink into your heart.

By studying the Biblical concepts of spiritually seeing and hearing (Isaiah 6:9-10, Ezekiel 12:2, Psalm 40:6, Proverbs 20:12, Matthew 13:10-16, John 8:43, Hebrews 5:11, Acts 28:27), we sadly find God's people, the Jews, growing blind and dull of really hearing what God was trying to say to them. From Luke 14:35 and other Scriptures, it is obvious that the Church is doing the same as we approach the end of this age and the time of His great wedding feast. The last statement to each and every one of the seven churches in Revelations 2 and 3 was, *He that hath an ear, let him hear what the spirit saith to the churches.* He exhorts each church—each individual—to **hear** and to <u>overcome</u> whatever obstacles they face in their individual situations. I believe He tells each of us to **overcome** the barriers to Him in our lives, whatever their nature, and prepare to meet our Lord in the air.

The Scriptures that we have studied are piercing and challenging. We can do one of two things with all of these Scriptures. One, we could dismiss all of these warnings as being too hard for us. This is what many followers said about Christ's teaching concerning His needed blood sacrifice for them in John 6:48-68; they said: *"This is a hard teaching. Who can accept [hear—KJV] it?"* (John 6:60b—NIV). They then walked away from following Christ! Or second, we can react to Christ's teachings in a correct way as Peter did when he said, *"Lord, to whom shall we go? You have the words of eternal life."* (John 6:68—NIV).

Over one-third of this book, as you have now discovered, is pure Scripture. You probably had no previous idea that so many Scriptures and concepts were related to the Rapture. These are not my words, but as Paul said in 1 Thessalonians

2:13b (NIV): *"...when you received the word of God, which you heard from us, you accepted it not as a human word, but as it actually is, **the word of God,** which is indeed at work in you who **believe.** * All of Scripture is for our good and our growth. 2 Timothy 3:16-17: [16] *All scripture is given by inspiration of God, and is profitable for doctrine, for reproof, for correction, for instruction in righteousness:* [17] *That the man of God may be perfect, thoroughly furnished unto all good works.* Yes, the Word of God is likened unto a sword or scalpel. Hebrews 4:12 (NIV): *For the word of God is alive and active. Sharper than any double-edged sword, it penetrates even to dividing soul and spirit, joints and marrow; it judges the thoughts and attitudes of the heart.* Let the Great Physician operate on us, cutting out the rubbish, and heal us body, soul, and spirit.

If it seems that some of my exhortations have been too sharp, I cannot apologize. [17b] *...we shall be caught up together with him in the clouds, to meet the Lord in the air, and so shall we ever be with the Lord.* [18] *Wherefore, comfort one another with these words* (1 Thessalonians 4:17b-18). Again, recall what comfort means: to desire, to invite, to call for, invoke, implore, beseech, exhort. These are powerful action verbs which I have tried to fulfill in my desire for others to fully comprehend all that Jesus and the Holy Spirit has spoken concerning His coming and His deeper will for our lives.

We must see our **Loving Father** in heaven calling us, wooing us, and warning us, because He wants us to be faithful and to be ready for His Son. He wants no one to perish or miss their heavenly home. We can let these Scriptures bring a healthy **fear of the Lord** into our lives to change our lives for the better. Psalm 55:19b says: *Because they have no changes, therefore they fear not God.* We should be inspired and spurred on by all of these Scriptures and by our love for our Bridegroom to prepare, to fill our lamps, and to set a watch. We must cast off sloth and the cares of this world, and focus on the eternal kingdom of God. These Scriptures should stir us up to live as if today is the last day of our life on this earth.

The very last thing Jesus said to the Church in Revelation 3:20 was: *Behold, I stand at the door, and knock: if any man hear my voice, and open the door, I **will come** in to him, and will sup with him, and he with me.* We often interpret this well-known verse as Christ calling to unsaved sinners. However, this verse was given to the lukewarm, deceived, Laodicean church, which represents the end-time church age; He found himself on the outside of that church, wanting individuals to open the door of their heart to Him once again. He so wants us to open up to Him. He wants us to sit down at that great marriage supper with Him. *Come,* he says to the Bride. *Come.*

Will you come? Will you hear? Will you take heed? Will you stop and take time? Will you be a faithful and wise servant? Will you watch like a soldier and look for Him? Will you be sober and vigilant? Will you keep your garments or spirit clean and live righteously before Him? Will you hold fast and persevere? Will you fear and love the Lord enough to make changes in your life?

Hearing all these things, *What manner of persons ought we to be?* (2 Peter 3:11b)

Agree with me in prayer—I say *yes* to these questions. Yes, I will awaken. Yes, I will hear. Yes, I will repent. Yes, I will be wise. Yes, I will live a sober, righteous and godly life. Yes, I will hold fast and persevere. Yes, I will set a watch. Yes, I will take heed. Yes, I will be faithful. Yes, I will fear the Lord and make changes and not excuses. Yes, God, I will put away things that get in the way of You. Yes, Lord, I will overcome. Yes, Lord, I decide to love you with all my heart, soul, mind, and strength; make me a faithful Bride, anticipating my soon-coming Bridegroom.

2 Timothy 4:8: *Henceforth there is laid up for me a crown of righteousness, which the Lord, the righteous judge, shall give me at that day: and not to me only, but unto all them also that **love his appearing.***

Our Lord's Last Plea

The Spirit and the Bride says "**come** *quickly, Lord Jesus.*"

Among Jesus' last words to us
in the very last chapter of the Bible are
Revelation 22:12, 17, and 20:

¹² *And, behold, I* **come** *quickly;*
and my reward is with me,
to give every man
according as his work shall be.
¹⁷ *And the Spirit and the bride say,*
Come.
And let him that heareth say,
Come.
And let him that is athirst
come.
And whosoever will,
let him take the water of life freely.

The second to the last verse in the Bible says:

²⁰ *Surely I* **come** *quickly. Amen.*
Even so, **come,** *Lord Jesus.*

Come join the Bride and the Bridegroom
At the Wedding Supper of the Lamb!

Discussion Questions

I. What is the Rapture?

1. Which two groups of saints shall be "caught up" and/or raptured?

2. What two Old Testament characters were "caught up" into heaven and never experienced death?

3. List two or three qualities or characteristics given for why God raptured one of the above people.

4. Discuss several differences between the Rapture and Christ's Second Coming.

5. ...*comfort one another with these words*—Give your four favorite concordance translations of the word *comfort*.

6. Discuss why everyone—Christian or not—needs to understand the Rapture.

II. How Will the Rapture Be Accomplished?

7. What immediately happens to the physical bodies of believers who are resurrected or raptured?

8. Discuss 1 John 3:1-3.

9. What would you pay in percentage of income or total wealth (if you could) for a glorious resurrection body? What is the real spiritual price of such a resurrection body?

10. What does Scripture mean when it says ...*that they might obtain a better resurrection*?

III. Where Will the Rapture Occur?

11. Up until the 3rd decade A.D., a Rapture would only have affected people in or near _____ because all early believers were _____.

12. Choose your four favorite bolded words or phrases which explain where the Rapture will occur.

IV. Two Reasons Why There Will Be a Rapture

13. God the Father says that He is married unto _____. Who are the Bridegroom and the Bride mentioned in Scripture?

14. Discuss the *great mystery* of Ephesians 5:25-27 and 32.

15. From John 14:1-3 <u>and</u> 1 Corinthians 2:9, can you describe your mansion or abode in heaven?

16. What four key principles are the most important concepts that you take with you personally from the Eastern Wedding Customs studies?

17. Abraham teaches us what principle about God's righteous judgment?

18. What must we learn from Lot and Lot's wife?

V. WHEN—Truths Concerning the Timing of the Rapture

19. What is the most important "rule" to always remember concerning the timing of the Rapture?

20. Which four of 2 Timothy 3:1-7's list of 20 perilous days' signs do you believe have affected you personally or are the most dangerous?

21. Which two of Christ's nine signs in Matthew 24:3-14 preceding His coming have affected you the most personally? Which have affected our nation the most? Which have affected the world the most?

22. Who or what is the fig tree blossoming in the end times as a sign to the world?

23. Give several negative results or reasons why we would not want to fight against what God is doing in the end times through His chosen people and land as a sign to the world (Isaiah 41:8-20). What positive things will God do for them?

24. Explain what the *fellowship of the mystery* means to you. Explain what or who is a fellowcitizen of the Commonwealth of Israel.

25. Compare Noah's time period to our own.

26. List six characteristics of Noah that brought the grace of God to his and his family's lives.

27. How is the ark a possible foreshadowing of the Rapture?

28. Why has the Father delayed the Rapture? Can the Church hurry up the timing?

29. Concerning the delay of the Rapture, what attitude do we need to take? Concerning the delay, what attitude do we need to avoid?

30. What does the phrase *come as a thief in the night* mean to you?

31. What restrains or holds back the Anti-Christ from being revealed or loosed on the earth until the time it is taken out of the way?

32. Discuss what God says He will do for the Church concerning the *wrath to come* or the *trials or time of Great Tribulation.*

33. Why is the Church not mentioned in Revelation after Chapter 5? Therefore, who has to witness to the world during the Great Tribulation?

VI. Who Will Be Raptured?

34. The summary pages of **Who Will Be Raptured** are really qualities, _____, or _____ given throughout this book of those who will be _____.

35. Analyze and discuss these pages of composite qualities of the Bride.

36. It is vital that we remember that these qualities or characteristics are not works of the _____, but are _____ of the Spirit.

37. Do you think 2 Timothy 4:3-4 is happening today? Does this book, therefore, go against the spirit of the time?

38. If Christians are saved and raptured out of this world's judgment, will Christians ever be judged? Discuss what is said in Romans 14:10b-12, 2 Corinthians 5:10-11a, 1 Corinthians 3:1-15, and Matthew 16:27.

39. What is the purpose of the [bema] judgment seat of Christ?

40. List the Scriptures or parables that speak about half of certain groups of believers being ready and taken.

41. What are the virgins' and the oil's significance in the Parable of the Ten Virgins?

42. Discuss wise versus unwise—servants, builders, and virgins. Comment on Christ telling the unwise: *I know you not.*

43. In the natural, why should the word "watch" (or "looking for") actually bother us? Explain several possible answers to that quandary.

44. Divide the ten martial or military-related mentalities or analogies among your group—comment on these and, if you can, add further corresponding Scriptures to each. If military, law enforcement, or security personnel are present, ask for their insights.

45. See if you can add further comparisons or analogies to the military mentality of "watch." [Example: The power or authority Christians have in the name of Jesus compared to the authority that a uniform or a badge has when worn by a regular person.]

46. What did Nehemiah's people have to do in order to re-build Jerusalem?

47. What areas of worldly excuses were made in the Parable of the Great Wedding Supper?

48. How angry did God become? What did God do?

49. Jesus' last words to the churches of Asia Minor [Turkey] are found in Revelation 3:20. Compare this to His last words to us in Revelation 22: 12, 17, and 20.

50. Seeing (reading) all these things—*what manner of persons ought we to be?*

Final Challenge Question

I challenge you with an allegory. Are you personally more like a thermometer or a thermostat? Concerning Christ's imminent coming, how much fire do you have or should you have? If you do little or nothing after reading this book, then you are more like a thermometer which only reads and complains about the cold. If the answer is "I need more of the fire of God," then become like a thermostat; thermostats are connected to the source of the fire—to the furnace—the Holy Spirit. Call on the Holy Spirit to burn away the dross in your life and to light a fire in your spirit like never before. A fire can't help but spread the heat of your renewed bride-like first love for Christ (and His soon-coming) with all the people around you—family, friends, neighbors—everyone.

Author's Note

This study on the Rapture is one of twelve "Foundations" of Christianity classes that can be found on the website: www.bethelbiblical.org (in Lakewood, Colorado). Class sessions can be watched and pre-studies, outlines, and handouts can be downloaded.

These classes begin with basic salvation concepts and strengthen Scriptural understanding of our Christian walk. The last three lessons are prophetic in nature. This topic of the Rapture has come out of Lesson 10 in that series.

There are also two sermons that I taught at Bethel Biblical which have been placed after the Foundations Classes and are available on that portion of website. They are entitled: *Israel's Spring Feasts—Christ's Fulfillment* (April 20, 2011), and *Fall Feasts of Israel* (September 7, 2011). In Christ's First Coming, He has already completely fulfilled all three of the spring feasts in His death, burial, and resurrection. God has also fulfilled the summer feast of Pentecost; it was fulfilled with the outpouring of the Holy Spirit on the Day of Pentecost. He will also fulfill all three of the fall feasts in the three events of the Rapture, the tribulation, and the Second Coming. Since the Rapture is foreshadowed in the first fall Feast of Trumpets/Teruah/or Rosh Hashanah, it would be an added blessing and revelation to you to see how God's feasts reveal future events like the Rapture of the Church. It especially speaks to the timing—the "**When**" of God's coming.

There is also a third sermon entitled: *The Watchmen* (October 27, 2010) which has to do with our key command: to **watch** for the Rapture.

If you or anyone you know desires more Christian foundational studies, please feel free to take these classes which I teach online. All weekly sermons given at Bethel Biblical are also available online.

May God bless you as you strengthen and sharpen your spiritual understanding and love for Him!

Chuck Mummert

MARANATHA!

The Lord Is Coming!

Appendix

**Listing of Scriptures Quoted
in each Section of this Book:**

[Partially quoted or referenced Scriptures are not listed]

I. What is the Rapture?

1 Thess. 4:16-18	2 Kings 2:11
Gen. 5:24	1 Cor. 10:11
Heb. 11:5	Heb. 10:23-25

II. How Will the Rapture Be Accomplished?

1 Thess. 4:16-17	1 John 3:1-3
1 Cor. 15:35-44, 52-58	Heb. 11:35b

III. Where Will the Rapture Occur?

Matt. 28:19	Acts 10:34-35
Acts 1:8b	Isa. 49:6b, 22a
Acts 2:21b	Rev. 5:9b
Acts 10:28b	

IV. Two Reasons Why There Will Be a Rapture

Matt. 22:37-38	Isa. 54:5
Deut. 6:5	Hosea 2:19-20
Jer. 3:14	John 3:28b-30

Matt. 9:14-15	2 Cor. 11:2
Rom. 7:4	Rev. 19:7
Matt. 22:29	1 Thess. 4:18
Gal. 3:26, 28-29	1 Cor. 2:9
2 Cor. 11:2	Matt. 24:21
Eph. 5:25-27, 32	Isa. 26:19-21
John 14:1-3	Zeph. 2:2-3
1 Cor. 2:9	Ps. 89:14
Rev. 19:7-9	Rom. 11:22a
Matt. 26:28-29	Deut. 10:12-13
1 Pet. 1:18-19	1 Cor. 10:11-12
1 Cor. 10:16a	Gen. 18:23, 25
Matt. 1:18-19	Ps. 97:2b
John 14:2-3	Ps. 96:10b, 13
2 Cor. 5:7	2 Pet. 2:6-8
1 Pet. 1:8	Luke 17:32
Matt. 24:36	Matt. 7:13-14

V. WHEN—Truths Concerning the Timing of the Rapture

Matt. 24:36, 42	Matt. 24:32-34
Mark 13:32-37	Song 2:4, 10, 13
Matt. 25:13	Isa. 41:8-20
Matt. 16:2-3	Joel 3:1-2
2 Tim. 3:1-7	Ps. 120:7
John 14:6a	Ps. 83:1-4
Luke 21:25-26	Ps. 102:13, 16
Rev. 6:9-10	Ps. 122:6
Rom. 8:18-23	Eph. 2:13-16a, 19-20

Rom. 3:29-30

Eph. 3:9

Ruth 1:16b

Rom. 11:1a, 17-27

Ps. 105:8-11

Isa. 54:5-10

Isa. 66:22

Matt. 24:36-39

Luke 10:38-42

Matt. 4:4

Gen. 6:3a, 5-9, 22

Heb. 11:7

Matt. 24:40-41, 42-51

Matt. 25:5, 19

James 5:7-8, 9b

Matt. 9:37-38

Matt. 24:14

2 Pet. 3:3-4, 8-10a, 11b

Luke 18:1-8

1 Thess. 5:1-23

Rev. 3:2-3

Rev. 1:7

1 Thess. 3:13b

Jude 1:14b-15a

Col. 3:4

Zech. 14:1-9

John 16:33

Matt. 24:21

Rev. 6:15-17

2 Thess. 2:1-12

John 16:7b-13a

2 Thess. 2:8

Rev. 19:20

Rom. 5:9

1 Thess. 1:10

1 Thess. 5:9

Luke 21:34-36

Rev. 3:10-11

Rev. 4:1

1 Thess. 4:16-17

Rev 5:9

Rev. 14:6

Rom. 1:18

Rev. 2:23

Rev. 2:5a

Rev. 3:10

Luke 21:36

1 Thess. 5:9

VI. Who Will Be Raptured?

Matt. 7:16

Phil. 1:9-11

Rom. 7:4

2 Pet. 3:11b-12a

Luke 8:14-15, 8b, 18a	Phil. 1:21
John 15:1-5, 8	2 Tim. 2:3-4
Rev. 21:27	1 Cor. 16:13
Gal. 5:19-21, 24	2 Tim. 2:15
2 Tim. 3:5	2 Cor. 5:17
John 3:3	Phil. 2:3-4
Matt. 18:3	2 Cor. 6:14a
Heb. 4:12b-13	1 Pet. 5:8
Matt. 22:37-38	Prov. 8:34
Matt. 24:40-41	Col. 3:2
2 Tim. 4:3-4	Prov. 29:18
Eph. 2:8-10	1 Thess. 5:6
Matt. 7:21-27	Col. 4:2
Rom. 14:10b-12	1 Cor. 6:19b
2 Cor. 5:10-11a	Prov. 6:10-11a
Matt. 25:1-13	Eph. 6:10-13, 18
2 Tim. 3:5	2 Tim. 2:3
2 Cor. 4:16b	Neh. 4:7-9, 13-18
Rom. 3:11b-14	Neh. 7:3b
Eph. 5:14, 15	Luke 14:16-35
Ex. 23:13	Matt. 22:11-14
Deut. 30:6	Matt. 16:24-27
Eph. 5:16-18, 25-27	Rev. 2:2-5
Mark 13:32-37	John 6:60b, 68
Rev. 16:15a	1 Thess. 2:13b
2 Pet. 3:12a, 14	2 Tim. 3:16-17
Titus 2:12-13	Heb. 4:12
Heb. 9:28	1 Thess. 4:17b-18

Ps. 55:19b

Rev. 3:20

2 Pet. 3:11b

2 Tim. 4:8

Rev. 22:12, 17, 20

CPSIA information can be obtained
at www.ICGtesting.com
Printed in the USA
FSOW02n1718180815
10044FS